A BEGINNER'S GUIDE TO THE

INDIAN STOCK MARKET

A BEGINNER'S GUIDE TO THE
INDIAN STOCK MARKET

LEARN | INVEST | GROW

KARTHIK RANGAPPA

HARPER

NON-FICTION

An Imprint of HarperCollins *Publishers*

First published in India by Harper Non-Fiction 2026
An imprint of HarperCollins *Publishers*
HarperCollins Publishers India, Cyber City,
Building 10-A, Gurugram, Haryana – 122002, India
www.harpercollins.co.in

2 4 6 8 10 9 7 5 3 1

P-ISBN: 978-93-6989-876-3
E-ISBN: 978-93-6989-377-5

Typeset in 12 pt/16 Minion Pro
by HarperCollins *Publishers* India Pvt. Ltd

Printed and bound at
Repro India Limited

This book is produced from independently certified FSC® paper to ensure responsible forest management.

*

HarperCollins *Publishers*, Macken House, 39/40 Mayor Street Upper, Dublin 1, D01 C9W8, Ireland

To my parents, for never giving up on me
To my wife, Ashwini, for always being there for me
To Zerodha, for showing me that businesses can be
built with heart.

Contents

Foreword

When we started Zerodha in 2010, we quickly realized something: Most people entering the stock markets had no idea what they were doing. Not because they weren't smart or capable, but because there was barely any good, accessible educational content in India.

What little existed was either locked behind expensive courses, buried in overly academic textbooks or peddled by people more interested in selling trading tips than actually teaching. The few resources that were free often made simple concepts sound impossibly complex, as if confusion was somehow proof of sophistication.

This gap was dangerous and personally frustrating to me. People were jumping into markets with real money, making decisions based on tips from WhatsApp groups or TV shows, with no understanding of what they were actually doing or why. The outcomes were predictable.

People lost money, blamed the markets and walked away convinced that investing was either a scam or only for the wealthy and well-connected.

We started Varsity in 2014 to change this. The idea was straightforward: Create honest, comprehensive educational content that takes someone from knowing absolutely nothing to being reasonably informed. No jargon or unrealistic promises, no hidden agenda. Just the fundamentals of how markets work, explained clearly and made freely available to anyone with an internet connection. We believed an informed investor is the best customer we could have for Zerodha.

This book is based on the first module of Varsity—*Introduction to Stock Markets*. The module helped millions of people start their investing journey, and I'm glad to see it reach even more people through this HarperCollins India edition.

But let me be clear: This book won't make you a stock market expert overnight. It won't give you a secret formula for picking winning stocks. The markets are complex and learning to navigate them takes time, practice and quite a bit of trial and error, much like any other profession. Anyone who tells you otherwise is probably trying to sell you something.

What this book *will* do is give you a solid foundation. You'll understand what stocks are, how markets function, who the key participants are and what happens when you place a trade. You'll learn the basic vocabulary and frameworks that every investor needs. Think of it like learning the rules of a sport before you start playing: You still need to develop strategy and skill, but at least you'll know how everything works.

A few things I've learned over the years that might help as you read this.

First, don't rush. Take your time with each concept. The market will still be there tomorrow. The best investors I know built understanding gradually and didn't risk money they couldn't afford to lose while learning.

Second, be sceptical of anyone promising quick riches or guaranteed returns. Markets don't work that way. If you come across something that sounds too good to be true, it almost certainly is.

Third, remember that financial education isn't a one-time thing. Markets evolve, regulations change and your own understanding deepens with experience.

This book is a starting point. Varsity has many more modules covering everything from technical analysis to options trading to personal finance—all free, and always will be.

Finally, investing is a long-term game. The stock market isn't a casino, and it's not a place to make quick money for next month's rent. It's a way to participate in the growth of businesses and the economy over years and decades. The sooner you internalize this, the better your chances of success.

I hope this book serves you well. Good luck.

Nithin Kamath
Founder and Chief Executive Officer, Zerodha

Introduction

My first job

It was February 2001, and I had just received my very first salary cheque for ₹5,000. Even back then, this didn't feel like much, considering most campus jobs offered monthly salaries in the ₹18,000 to ₹20,000 range. But this ₹5,000 felt incredibly special to me. It was the very first time I had earned a salary.

I wanted to do four things with this money:

- Buy my parents something nice
- Buy my girlfriend (now my wife) a thoughtful gift
- Party with a few good friends
- Save some money

I know I was being overly ambitious with a mere ₹5,000, but that's how life felt back then. 😊

While the first three goals sound intuitive, you might wonder if it was even possible to save anything meaningful from just ₹5,000. I was in my early twenties, Bangalore had new bars and restaurants opening on every corner, and weekend parties were the norm. Why did I want to save such a small amount? Why not just have fun now and save when I was earning more substantially?

The foundation

My parents maintained busy schedules throughout their working years, until they retired in the 2000s. They both banked with Corporation Bank (now Union Bank of India), which had a branch just twenty steps from our house—literally.

My parents lived by monthly budgets and spent very little beyond the essentials. This wasn't because they were miserly, but, rather, they understood the weight of financial security. Every purchase was measured against future needs, and every rupee saved felt like a small victory against uncertainty. They would allocate money for household expenses and save the rest in their bank account. They visited the bank regularly to deposit cheques, and whenever they were pressed for time, they would send me on these banking errands.

I'd hand over the cheque to the bank manager, who happened to be a family friend. He would guide me through filling out the bank slips and dropping the cheque into the wooden 'cheque box'.

While I understood little about what I was actually doing, these tasks always filled me with a deep sense of responsibility. I loved these 'bank jobs', even though I never fully grasped the mechanics behind them.

But I understood one fundamental thing—as soon as money comes in, it needs to go into the bank. This principle became ingrained in my thinking early in life.

The different path

Fast-forward to 2001. When I received my first salary cheque of ₹5,000, I knew I had to save something, regardless of how big or small that amount might be. But being young and rebellious, I didn't want to follow my parents' playbook. I wanted to do something different—save my money somewhere other than a traditional bank account.

I approached my boss, Chandrashekar (now a very dear friend of mine), and asked him about alternative ways to save money. He was initially surprised by my question—after all, he knew exactly how much he was paying me! 😅

After the usual back-and-forth, he suggested I explore the stock market. That was the first time I'd heard the term 'stock market'. Chandra directed me to a broker's website to read some articles, hoping this would give me a quick start.

I tried, but gave up after just a few hours. The information was scattered, unhelpful and drowning in jargon.

I've never understood why people complicate finance with unnecessary jargon. The author Morgan Housel captures this perfectly in his statement: 'Finance is actually very simple, but it's made to look complicated to justify fees.'

The struggle begins

I made several attempts to get started with the stock market and kick-start my investment journey, but every step felt monumental. First, I had to understand how stock markets actually work. Then came setting up trading and DEMAT accounts, linking bank accounts and deciphering multiple order types. It was all overwhelming.

My attempt to learn about stock markets was plagued by both complexity and, admittedly, my own procrastination. It took me a full four years before I finally opened my first trading and DEMAT account.

The first trade

As soon as I opened my trading account, I called a friend who was working at Tata Consultancy Services

(TCS) on a software project for a major stock exchange. Predictably, I asked him which stock I should buy. My reasoning was simple—he was working on a stock exchange project, so he must know something.

Here's the thing about people and stock tips: If you ask for one, you'll definitely get one. Perhaps it's because people have an inherent desire to demonstrate knowledge that others don't possess. Anyway, my friend recommended two stocks: Sterling Biotech and FDC Limited.

I promptly bought both without questioning anything. I invested about ₹15,000 in each, and I remember being incredibly excited about these purchases.

Of course, I started tracking the stocks hourly. Every 50-paisa uptick felt like a major victory, and I was convinced these two stocks would be my gateway to a stock market rags-to-riches story.

Reality hits

The stocks performed reasonably well for the first few days. During this period, I enthusiastically shared my 'winning' stock market bets with anyone who would listen. Then the inevitable happened—both stocks dropped by 15 to 20 per cent from my entry points.

I was in disbelief. I panicked. I was nearly in tears. I desperately wanted my money back and seriously considered returning to my childhood bank manager to park everything in a fixed deposit.

But I'm glad I didn't panic-sell.

The real education begins

When the panic subsided and I regained some emotional control, I started asking the right questions: Why did my stocks fall? What caused the panic? How can I protect myself in the future?

That loss in Sterling Biotech and FDC Limited sparked my curiosity and led me to start learning in earnest about stocks and markets. There's a saying in the markets: 'Treat your losses as your "guru dakshina" for your stock market education.' The only difference is that the stock market collects this tuition fee upfront. 😊

Since that first purchase, I've been continuously learning about markets, constantly seeking answers. Over time, I've realized this is a never-ending journey. It took me several years just to get the basics right.

Life took many unexpected turns after the Sterling Biotech and FDC days. I had many adventures and fun while learning about stock markets along the way. Eventually, I joined Zerodha Broking Limited in 2014. Interestingly, from the very beginning, Nithin Kamath (the founder and CEO of Zerodha) envisioned capital market education as a core offering of Zerodha.

I consider myself incredibly privileged to have had the opportunity to build this education piece for Zerodha. Since 2014, I've been working on building Zerodha Varsity—a free and open-source learning platform dedicated to teaching trading and investing to individuals interested in capital markets.

Zerodha Varsity now has millions of users, and many of them have built careers in finance, made their first investments, bought their first mutual funds and placed their first trades by reading through Varsity.

To this day, I find this fact deeply humbling.

Why this book?

Thanks to Zerodha Varsity, over the years, I've interacted with hundreds of thousands of people, answering their queries related to stock markets. These interactions have happened both online and offline, across different age groups and across the country. Collectively, I've answered over 1,00,000 queries in the last twelve years. This experience has given me a clear sense of the common concerns people have about stock markets and where they typically get stuck in their thinking.

Keeping these interactions and learnings in perspective, I've created a structured learning path in this book that can fast-track your stock market education. I've organized it in a way that makes sense for systematic learning, focusing on helping you understand the market ecosystem and become comfortable with basic terminology.

Think of this book as your stepping stone to India's stock market.

CHAPTER 1

Why Should I Invest?

To understand stock markets, we need to take a step back and consider a perhaps more fundamental question: Why invest?

When we have money, the obvious urge is to spend it, especially for young people, perhaps in the first few years of salaried life. That new pair of sneakers, that new set of AirPods, that new phone, that new handbag—the list goes on.

Somehow, saving for retirement or for any financial goal doesn't really feature anywhere. Understandably so, especially if you are young, leading a carefree life, and have zero or very limited responsibilities. It's easy to believe that life will continue the same way.

But unfortunately, it does not. Life happens, and circumstances, especially financial circumstances, change, and you need to be financially prepared for that.

To help you understand this, let's assume for a moment that we all live in a simple world. We earn some money, spend part of it on our day-to-day expenses and whatever is left piles up somewhere.

This 'somewhere' could be a bank account that yields almost no returns today. Let's put some numbers to this for better clarity.

Assume you earn ₹50,000 per month and spend ₹30,000 on your day-to-day living expenses; these expenses can include things like housing, food, transport, shopping, medical needs, etc. The balance of ₹20,000 is your monthly surplus.

As I mentioned earlier, let's assume we live in a simple world; therefore, let's forget taxes and some real-world practicalities for a moment. I promise, this is the only time in the entire book that I'll let go of the practicalities of life.

While we're at it, I'll also make a few assumptions:

- Your employer is kind enough to give you a 10 per cent salary hike every year.
- The cost of living is likely to go up by 8 per cent yearly.
- You are thirty years old and plan to retire at fifty, which translates to twenty working years.
- You don't intend to work after you retire.
- Your expenses are fixed, and you don't foresee any other expenses.
- The balance cash of ₹20,000 per month is retained as hard cash.

Going by these assumptions, this is what your cash balance will look like in twenty years:

WITHOUT INVESTMENTS

Years	Yearly Income	Yearly Expenses	Cash Retained
1	600,000	360,000	240,000
2	660,000	388,800	271,200
3	726,000	419,904	306,096
4	798,600	453,496	345,104
5	878,460	489,776	388,684
6	966,306	528,958	437,348
7	1,062,937	571,275	491,662
8	1,169,230	616,977	552,254
9	1,286,153	666,335	619,818
10	1,414,769	719,642	695,127
11	1,556,245	777,213	779,032
12	1,711,870	839,390	872,480
13	1,883,057	906,541	976,516
14	2,071,363	979,065	1,092,298
15	2,278,499	1,057,390	1,221,109
16	2,506,349	1,141,981	1,364,368
17	2,756,984	1,233,339	1,523,644
18	3,032,682	1,332,006	1,700,676
19	3,335,950	1,438,567	1,897,383
20	3,669,545	1,553,652	2,115,893
		Total Income	17,890,693

Here is how to read this table: In the first year, you earn ₹6 lakh in income, your yearly expenses are ₹3.6 lakh, and the balance of ₹2.4 lakh is retained in your bank.

In the second year, you get an increment of 10 per cent, so you earn ₹6.6 lakh. Your expenses increase by 8 per cent, so you spend ₹3.88 lakh, and the balance of ₹2.71 lakh is retained in your bank account. At the end of twenty years, the sum total of the cash retained gives you the total money in your account, which you will probably utilize for your retirement.

If you look at the table carefully, it is a scary situation. A few things are obvious:

- After twenty years of hard work, you have accumulated ₹1.7 crore.

- Since your expenses are fixed, your lifestyle has not changed over the years, and you have probably even suppressed your lifelong aspirations—a better home, car, vacations, etc.

- After you retire, assuming expenses continue to grow at 8 per cent, the retirement corpus of ₹1.7 crore is good enough to sail you through roughly eight years of post-retirement life. From the eighth year onwards, you will be in a very tricky spot with literally no savings left to back you up.

What will you do after you run out of money in eight years? How will you fund your life? Is there a way to ensure that you accumulate a larger corpus at the end of twenty years? At this point, you may think this example is too simple and that real life doesn't work like this. I agree, and I won't dispute that fact.

However, the point to note in the above calculation is that no investments are made; hence, the cash retained has flat or zero growth.

Let's consider another scenario where, instead of keeping the cash idle, you choose to invest it in an investment option that grows at, let's say, 12 per cent per annum. For example, in the first year, you retained ₹2,40,000, which, when invested at 12 per cent per annum for twenty years (nineteen years, assuming you invest at the end of the first year), yields ₹20,67,063 at the end of the twentieth year.

For those interested in math, here's how that works:

2,40,000 * (1 + 12%) ^ (19) = 20,67,063

Don't worry about the math at this point, we'll deal with it later in the book. For now, just know that the formula used above helps you understand the value of money when it grows at a certain rate of return (12 per cent in this case) over a certain period of time (nineteen years in this case).

If you apply the same across all the years, here is how the table looks:

WITH INVESTMENTS

Years	Yearly Income	Yearly Expenses	Cash Retained	Retained Cash Invested at 12%
1	600,000	360,000	240,000	2,067,063
2	660,000	388,800	271,200	2,085,519
3	726,000	419,904	306,096	2,101,668
4	798,600	453,496	345,104	2,115,621
5	878,460	489,776	388,684	2,127,487
6	966,306	528,958	437,348	2,137,368
7	1,062,937	571,275	491,662	2,145,363
8	1,169,230	616,977	552,254	2,151,566
9	1,286,153	666,335	619,818	2,156,069
10	1,414,769	719,642	695,127	2,158,959
11	1,556,245	777,213	779,032	2,160,318
12	1,711,870	839,390	872,480	2,160,228
13	1,883,057	906,541	976,516	2,158,765
14	2,071,363	979,065	1,092,298	2,156,003
15	2,278,499	1,057,390	1,221,109	2,152,012
16	2,506,349	1,141,981	1,364,368	2,146,859
17	2,756,984	1,233,339	1,523,644	2,140,611
18	3,032,682	1,332,006	1,700,676	2,133,328
19	3,335,950	1,438,567	1,897,383	2,125,069
20	3,669,545	1,553,652	2,115,893	2,115,893
		Total Income	17,890,693	42,695,771

Notice that the final cash balance, or the corpus, has increased significantly. The decision to invest has clearly helped. The cash balance has grown to ₹4.26 crore from ₹1.7 crore, a staggering 2.4x more than earlier (when you choose not to invest).

Now, let's circle back and understand why one should invest, a question we asked right at the start. Clearly, there are a few compelling reasons:

- **Fight inflation:** Inflation, as you may have heard a million times before, is the process by which money loses its purchasing power. What you can buy for ₹100 today will cost ₹105 next year. One way to beat and manage inflation is by investing in assets that tend to generate returns higher than inflation.

- **Create wealth:** By investing, one can build a bigger corpus by the end of the target period. In the above example, the period was up to retirement, but it can be anything—children's education, marriage, buying a house, holidays, etc.

- **A better life:** To meet life's financial aspirations.

Hopefully, I have given you enough context to help you understand why you should consider investing.

Where to invest?

Having figured out the reasons to invest, the next obvious questions are: Where should one invest, how much should one invest and what returns can one expect from different financial instruments?

When investing, one has to choose an asset class that suits the individual's risk and return profile. For example, one individual may be open to taking a lot of risk with their money, while another may prefer moderate risk, and another may want zero risk.

Think of an asset class as an investment vehicle defined by its risk and return characteristics. The following are some of the popular asset classes:

- Fixed income instruments
- Equity
- Real estate
- Gold and silver

For an individual in India, these are largely the available investment options. Usually, people skew their investments towards assets they are comfortable with. For example, someone who prefers or understands real estate will have more investment in real estate assets. In my own case, I'm comfortable with stocks, so I have more exposure to equity.

How much to invest, where and in what proportion is, in itself, a topic for another day. But for now, I'd like to give you a quick overview of what to expect from each of the four asset classes I've mentioned above.

Fixed-income instruments

Fixed-income instruments are somewhat like your bank fixed deposits (FDs). In fact, FDs are a subset of the larger fixed income instruments world. In a fixed-income instrument, your money is lent to an entity, which in turn assures you of the safety of your capital and pays you an interest amount.

The bank's fixed deposit scheme is the simplest example of a fixed-income instrument. The interest paid could be quarterly, semi-annual or annual. The capital is returned to the investor at the end of the investment period, also known as the maturity period. Fixed-income instruments are also commonly referred to as bonds.

A few examples of fixed-income instruments are:

- Bank fixed deposits

- Bonds issued by the Government of India (also called G-Sec bonds and T-Bills)

- Bonds issued by government-related agencies such as Gas Authority of India Limited (GAIL), Housing and Urban Development Corporation Limited

(HUDCO), National Highways Authority of India (NHAI), etc.

- Bonds issued by corporates (Tata, Bajaj, Reliance, Adani).

As of today, the typical return from a fixed-income instrument varies between 5 and 6 per cent. Government bonds offer about 5.5 per cent, and a few corporate bonds offer nearly 9 or 10 per cent. The rates across different instruments vary because the risk varies.

Government bonds are considered the safest investment, with zero risk to your investment, because, well, the government can't cheat and run away with your money. Corporate bonds, however, are riskier; investments in corporate bonds can go to zero, and we have seen plenty of such examples in the past.

Equity

Investment in equities involves buying shares of publicly listed companies. The shares are traded on the Bombay Stock Exchange (BSE) and the National Stock Exchange (NSE).

When an investor invests in equity, unlike a fixed-income instrument, there is no capital guarantee. However, as a trade-off, the returns from equity investment can be much better. Indian equities have generated upwards of 12 per cent returns year-on-year over the last two decades.

Investing in some of the best and most well-run Indian companies has yielded a compound annual growth rate (CAGR) of over 20 per cent in the long term. Identifying such investment opportunities requires skill, hard work and patience.

Real estate

Real estate investment involves transacting (buying and selling) commercial and non-commercial property. Typical examples include vacant plots, apartments and commercial buildings. There are two sources of income from real estate investments: Rental income and capital appreciation of the investment amount. The rental yield typically varies between 1.5 and 2 per cent, which is not very attractive, in my opinion. Appreciation in land prices occurs in select pockets, is not uniform and requires you to be deeply connected to local networks.

The transaction process can be quite complex, involving legal verification of documents. The cash outlay for real estate investments is usually quite large. There is no official metric to measure the returns generated by real estate. Hence, it is hard to comment on this.

A few real estate investment trusts (REITs) have emerged in India over the last few years. You can get exposure to commercial real estate through REITs. However, whether these REITs accurately reflect returns from the broader real estate market remains debatable.

Gold and silver

Gold and silver are among the most popular investment options. Over the long term, both have appreciated. Investments in these metals have yielded a CAGR of approximately 6 to 8 per cent over the last thirty years, and about 5 to 8 per cent over the last twenty years.

There are several ways to invest in gold and silver. One can invest in jewellery, exchange-traded funds (ETFs) or gold mutual funds. Between 2015 and 2025, there was also the option to invest in sovereign gold bonds (SGBs), but the government has now discontinued issuing these bonds.[1] Those already issued may still be trading on the exchange, but their pricing may not accurately reflect the true market price movement of gold.

Going back to our initial example of investing surplus cash, it would be interesting to see how much one would have saved by the end of twenty years by investing in any one of the asset classes—fixed income, equity or bullion.

---

1 'SGBs Discontinued in Budget 2025: What's the Best Way to Invest in Gold Now?', *Moneycontrol*, 5 February 2025, https://www.moneycontrol.com/news/business/personal-finance/sgbs-discontinued-in-budget-2025-what-s-the-best-way-to-invest-in-gold-now-12930675.html.

- By investing in fixed income at an average rate of 9 per cent per annum (a good corporate bond), the corpus would have grown to ₹3.3 crore.

- By investing in equities at an average rate of 15 per cent per annum, the corpus would have grown to ₹5.54 crore.

- By investing in bullion at an average rate of 8 per cent per annum, the corpus would have grown to ₹3.09 crore.

Equities tend to deliver the best returns, especially when you have a multi-year investment perspective.

Many of you reading this may wonder why I have not considered cryptocurrencies as an asset class. When you invest your hard-earned money, you need to ensure there are enough checks, balances and regulatory frameworks in place to protect you as an investor. Crypto lacks these; hence, I would suggest staying away from crypto (or any other fancy investment option) until a regulatory framework is established.

It is wise to diversify your investment across the various asset classes. The technique of allocating money across asset classes is termed 'asset allocation', and we will discuss this later.

As an example, a young professional may be able to take higher risk, given their age and the number of years available for investing. Typically, such investors should allocate at least 60 per cent of their investable amount to equity, 20 per cent to precious metals, and 20 per cent to fixed-income investments. This mix changes based on risk profile and age. For example, a retired person might invest 80 per cent in fixed income (government bonds, perhaps), 10 per cent in equity markets and 10 per cent in precious metals.

Stock markets

I hope by now you've noticed that there is no running away from equities, especially if you want to create wealth for yourself over the long run. There is more than enough research out there that points to this conclusion, so I'll stop arguing about what equities can do for you and your wealth-creation journey in the long term.

I'll assume I have established a case for equities. Having done that, in the rest of the book I'll focus on helping you get comfortable with stock markets, where equities are traded daily.

My goal is to help you understand the jargon, nuances and technicalities of the stock markets so you can comfortably make your first investment and kick-start your wealth-creation journey.

So buckle up and gear up for the ride.

Key takeaways

- One has to invest to secure one's financial future.

- The corpus you build at the end of the investment period is sensitive to the return percentage. Even a slight variation in the rate can significantly impact the final corpus.

- Choose an instrument that best suits your risk and return appetite.

- Equity should be a part of your investment if you want to beat inflation in the long run.

- A good investment practice is to build a portfolio that includes a mix of asset classes.

CHAPTER 2

What Is the Stock Market?

In the previous chapter, we established that investing in equities (stocks, mutual funds) is crucial for generating inflation-beating returns. Stocks and mutual funds will be your mission-critical components in the long-term wealth creation journey. This holds true for the thousands and millions of people investing in India every day.

Now, think of investing as a game—a long-term wealth creation game. If you were to play this game over multiple years, what would you consider the most important aspect? While you can probably generate a list of things that feel important, I'd put 'fair play' right at the top of that list. After all, you don't want to play this game over decades only to realize at the end that the rules were never in your favour. So, in that sense, fair play is very important.

However, fair play in terms of what, you may wonder? We'll get to that shortly. Before we delve deeper into this topic, it's essential to understand the market ecosystem and the many different entities involved in making our capital market journey smooth.

Just as we go to the neighbourhood kirana store or use quick commerce apps on our mobile phones to shop for daily needs, we go to the stock market to shop (or rather, transact) for investments. The stock market is where everyone who wishes to transact in securities goes.

The term 'securities' is a fancy word for common shares, mutual funds and various other financial instruments. In the context of stock markets, transacting means either buying or selling shares.

The primary purpose of the stock market is to facilitate transactions in securities. So, if you want to buy shares of a company, the stock market helps you meet the seller and vice versa.

Unlike a supermarket, the stock market doesn't exist in brick-and-mortar form. It exists electronically, much like a quick commerce app. You access the market electronically from your computer and carry out transactions (buy or sell). It's also important to note that you must access the stock market through a registered intermediary called a stockbroker. We'll discuss stockbrokers later.

'Stock market' is actually a collective term that includes all the stock exchanges operating in the country. Think of the stock market in the same way you think of an 'education system' in a country. Education system is a broad term that includes all the schools, colleges and universities operating in that country. Similarly, the stock market is a broad term that includes all the stock exchanges operating in the country.

Currently, India has two fully functioning stock exchanges—the Bombay Stock Exchange (BSE) and the National Stock Exchange (NSE). There were many other exchanges earlier, but only these two exist now. Older stock exchanges such as the Bangalore Stock Exchange (BgSE), Madras Stock Exchange (MSE) and Calcutta Stock Exchange (CSE) have either merged with BSE or NSE or shut down.

There is also the Multi-Commodity Exchange (MCX). As the name suggests, the MCX is where commodities such as gold, silver, crude oil and ferrous metals are transacted.

However, when you talk about stock markets in India, you are essentially referring to either the NSE or BSE, at least in the context of this book.

Market participants and the need to regulate them

The stock market attracts both individuals and institutions. The people who transact in the market—be it individuals like you and me or corporate entities—are collectively referred to as 'market participants'. There are different types of market participants:

- **Domestic retail participants:** People like you and me.

- **Non-resident Indians (NRIs) and overseas citizens of India (OCIs):** People of Indian origin who are based outside India.

- **Domestic institutions:** Homegrown corporate entities in India.

- **Domestic asset management companies (AMCs):** Mutual fund companies such as SBI Mutual Fund, HDFC AMC, Edelweiss, ICICI Prudential, Zerodha AMC, etc.

- **Portfolio management services (PMS):** Firms that offer investment services to wealthy individuals.

- **Alternative investment funds (AIFs):** These are the hedge fund equivalents in India. They usually take high-risk bets with the intent of making high returns. Currently, the minimum investment in an AIF is ₹1 crore, so this is clearly not for everyone.

- **Foreign institutional investors:** Non-Indian corporate entities such as foreign asset management companies, pension funds, sovereign wealth funds, hedge funds and other investors looking to invest in India

Now, regardless of who participates in the market, everyone's goal is to ensure every transaction is profitable—or, more bluntly put, to make money.

When money is involved, human emotions such as greed and fear tend to run high. One can easily fall prey to these emotions and get involved in unfair practices. India has had its fair share of episodes where people (and institutions) have engaged in unethical practices for bigger and quicker profits.

This isn't just true for India but for markets across the world as well. After all, when it comes to money, human emotions are largely the same, irrespective of where one comes from.

Given this, stock markets need someone who can set the rules of the game and mandate that everyone follows the same code of conduct. These sets of rules are commonly referred to as regulation and compliance.

If you're new to stock markets, it's super important to understand that you must abide by the rules governing them. However, there's a twist here. For a regular individual investor, it's almost impossible to keep track of all the rules and regulations. Compliance documents can run into several hundred pages. Besides, these regulations undergo regular changes and updates as the market evolves.

So how do you deal with this?

These regulations are largely meant for the intermediaries operating in the stock markets. As an individual, your job is to ensure that you deal only with intermediaries that are licensed to operate in the markets. For example, if you want stock market advice, make sure the person or agency providing it is regulated. Or, if you want to invest in a fund, ensure the fund is run by a proper fund management company holding the required licence.

This way, since the entity is regulated, it is forced to comply with fair-play rules and regulations and your interests are protected.

The regulator

Who sets these rules and regulations for stock markets? Who grants the required business licences to operate in the Indian markets? Well, the regulator does. Regulators are bestowed with these powers by the Government of India. In India, the stock market regulator is called the Securities and Exchange Board of India (SEBI).

SEBI aims to promote the development of stock exchanges, protect the interests of retail investors, and regulate the activities of market participants and financial intermediaries. In general, SEBI ensures that:

- Stock exchanges conduct their business fairly

- Stockbrokers conduct their business fairly

- Market participants do not engage in unfair practices

- Corporates don't use the markets to benefit only themselves

- Small investors' interests are protected
- Large investors with mega cash piles don't manipulate the markets
- Overall market development is encouraged

Given these objectives, it becomes imperative for SEBI to regulate all entities involved in the market. Based on the role an entity is expected to play, SEBI prescribes a set of rules and regulations applicable to that entity. Each entity must operate within the legal framework laid down by SEBI. These rules are made publicly available on SEBI's website. If you ever have an iota of doubt about the practices of a stock market entity, you can refer to SEBI's legal framework to determine whether the practice is legitimate.

Let me end this chapter by giving you a sense of the different entities involved in the stock markets (directly or indirectly) and their roles in the system.

MARKET ENTITIES

Entity	Example of companies	What do they do?	In simpler words
Credit rating agencies (CRAs)	Credit Rating Information Services of India Limited (CRISIL), Investment Information and Credit Rating Agency of India Limited (ICRA), Credit Analysis and Research Limited (CARE).	Rate the creditworthiness of corporates and governments.	If a corporate (or government) entity wants to avail a loan (debt financing), CRAs assess its creditworthiness and assign a rating. Based on this rating, other entities decide whether or not to extend a loan.

Entity	Example of companies	What do they do?	In simpler words
Debenture trustees	Almost all banks in India.	Act as trustees for corporate debentures.	When companies want to raise a loan, they can issue debentures against which they promise to pay interest. The public can subscribe to these debentures. A debenture trustee ensures that the company honours its debenture obligations.
Depositories	National Securities Depository (NSDL) and Central Depository Services (CDSL).	Ensure the safekeeping, reporting and settlement of clients' securities.	They act like a digital vault for your shares. This 'vault'—your depository account—is usually referred to as a dematerialized account, or DEMAT account. Depositories hold your shares and facilitate the exchange of your securities.

Entity	Example of companies	What do they do?	In simpler words
Depository participants (DP)	Most banks and stockbrokers.	Act as agents of the depositories.	You cannot directly interact with the NSDL or CDSL. You must liaise with a DP to open and maintain your DEMAT account.
Foreign institutional investors (FII)	Foreign corporates, funds and individuals.	Invest in Indian markets.	These are foreign entities that invest large sums of money in India. Their activity often impacts market sentiment.

Entity	Example of companies	What do they do?	In simpler words
Merchant bankers	Karvy, Axis Bank, Edelweiss Capital.	Help companies raise money in primary markets.	If a company plans to raise money through an initial public offering (IPO), merchant bankers manage and execute the IPO process.
Asset management companies (AMC)	HDFC AMC, Reliance Capital, SBI Capital, Zerodha AMC.	Offer mutual fund schemes.	AMCs collect money from the public (investors) and invest it in markets with the objective of growing the investments and generating wealth for investors.

Entity	Example of companies	What do they do?	In simpler words
Portfolio management services (PMS) and alternative investment funds (AIFs)	Capitalmind Wealth PMS, Motilal PMS, Parag Parikh PMS, 360 One, Avendus, Nuvama.	Offer PMS and AIF schemes.	Similar to mutual funds but with a higher minimum investment—₹50 lakh for PMS and ₹1 crore for AIFs. There are no such restrictions with AMCs—you can start as low as ₹100.
Stockbrokers	Zerodha, ICICI Direct, Groww, Motilal Oswal.	Act as intermediaries between investors and stock exchanges.	Stockbrokers act as a gateway to stock markets, providing electronic access to facilitate transactions.

If at this point you're confused by the number of entities and how they interact with each other, don't worry. At this stage, it's enough to know that these entities exist. Over the subsequent chapters, you'll gradually understand how they come together to form the stock market ecosystem. In fact, in the next chapter, I'd like to focus on a few of these entities and help you understand some of their nuances.

Key takeaways

- The stock market is the place where securities are transacted.

- Stock markets exist electronically and can be accessed through a stockbroker.

- There are many different market participants operating in the stock markets.

- SEBI is the regulator of the securities market in India. It sets the legal framework and regulates all entities interested in operating in the market.

- Every market entity must be regulated and can operate only within the framework prescribed by SEBI.

CHAPTER 3

Market Intermediaries

Did you watch the Brad Pitt-starrer *F1* (2025)? The film was spectacular, with never a dull moment. Now, would you attribute the success of the movie solely to Brad Pitt or Damson Idris? I hope not. While they are the faces of the movie, there are at least a dozen agencies working behind the scenes to make your movie-watching experience smooth and enjoyable. These agencies could be called 'movie intermediaries', whose job is to ensure your experience is seamless.

Similarly, we have 'market intermediaries'—a group of entities whose job is to work behind the scenes to ensure your experience of buying and selling shares is smooth when you transact in the stock market.

From the time you log into a trading terminal (say, to buy shares) to the time those shares appear in your DEMAT account, market intermediaries work seamlessly together to ensure your transactions go through without any hiccups.

These entities play their role quietly behind the scenes, always complying with the rules laid out by SEBI to ensure an effortless and smooth stock market experience. They are generally referred to as financial intermediaries or market infrastructure intermediaries (MIIs).

Together, these MIIs—interdependent on one another—create an ecosystem in which the financial markets operate. Let us now quickly review a few of these key market intermediaries and the roles they play in this ecosystem.

MIIs are largely categorized into three buckets:

- **Stock exchanges:** BSE, NSE, MCX and National Commodity and Derivatives Exchange

- **Depositories:** Central Depository Services Limited (CDSL), National Securities Depository Limited (NSDL)

- **Clearing corporations:** Indian Clearing Corporation Limited (ICCL), National Securities Clearing Corporation Limited (NSCCL), MCX Clearing Corporation Limited (MCX-CCL)

Besides these MIIs, we also have stockbrokers and banks. Together, these entities form the market ecosystem. In this chapter, I'd like to give you an overview of some of these entities and help you understand what they do.

The stockbroker

The stockbroker is probably one of the most important financial intermediaries you need to know. A stockbroker is a corporate entity registered as a trading member with a stock exchange and holds a stockbroking licence. SEBI grants this licence after thorough due diligence, and the broker is expected to comply with the rules prescribed by SEBI. These rules are constantly evolving as the market itself evolves.

A stockbroker is your gateway to the stock markets for making investments in stocks, bonds, ETFs and mutual funds. To transact in the stock market, you must set up an account with a stockbroker of your choice. These accounts are called the 'trading account' and the 'DEMAT account'. Most people get confused between the two and use them interchangeably. Please don't make that mistake—these are two different accounts, and they serve two different purposes.

Think of a trading account as your platform to buy and sell shares—let's say shares of Infosys. At the time of writing, Infosys was trading at ₹1,435 per share. Now, let's say you want to buy 100 shares at ₹1,430, which is ₹5 lower than the current trading price. You will need a trading account to specify your requirements—in this case, 100 shares of Infosys at ₹1,430 per share—and place the order.

Now, assume your order goes through and you acquire your 100 shares of Infosys. You decide these shares are earmarked for your grandkids, and you don't want to touch them for the next fifteen years. This means you need to store them safely somewhere, right?

You do this by holding them digitally in a DEMAT account.

So, very briefly, a trading account is primarily for order management, while a DEMAT account is for holding your shares or securities. We will get into more nuances later, but for now, please remember not to mistake a trading account for a DEMAT account, and vice versa.

A stockbroker helps you open both trading and DEMAT accounts. These two accounts seamlessly blend into the broker-provided platform, and you may not even realize that they are different. That's the magic of a good user interface (UI).

There are many registered stockbrokers in India, and you can choose one based on your preferences. A few popular filters that people use while selecting a stockbroker are:

- **Platform simplicity and reliability:** This is important as you will be using the broker's platform to place buy or sell orders.

- **Support system:** In case of any issue or confusion—which you will almost certainly have at the start of your investment journey—you need your problems resolved as quickly and accurately as possible.

- **Reports:** Remember, at the end of the year you will have to pay taxes. Ensure your broker provides reports that you can easily download and pass on to your chartered accountant (CA). I'm referring to reports such as profit & loss (P&L), tradebook, tax P&L, dividend reports, etc.

- **Net worth:** This refers to your broker's net worth. You don't want to deal with a broker who is not profitable or has weak financials. In fact, many broker-related frauds in India can be traced back to poor company finances. A broker with a strong net worth is less likely to commit fraud or engage in bad practices.

- **Charges:** Brokerage charges, DP charges, account opening charges, etc.

- **Education:** Check if your broker goes beyond basic services and engages in initiatives such as education. You will need this guidance, especially at the start of your investment journey.

Once you decide on your broker and open trading and DEMAT accounts, you can start transacting in the stock market. After setting up your account, there are a few standard ways to interact with your broker.

Call and Trade/Invest: You can call your broker, identify yourself using your client code (account code) and place an order. The dealer, at the other end, will execute the order for you and confirm its status while you are still on the call. This was the primary way people transacted until the mid-2000s. The practice still exists, but the number of people using this method has reduced significantly.

Do-it-yourself: This is perhaps the most popular way to transact in the markets. The broker gives you access to the market via a trading platform. After you log in, you can view live market prices and place orders yourself.

Programatic Market Access: Advanced users can access the market programmatically via the broker's application programming interface (API). Some brokers provide APIs for a fee.

Do note that the broker charges a fee for the services provided, also called the 'brokerage charge' or simply 'brokerage'. Brokerage rates vary, and it's up to you to find a broker that strikes the right balance between the charges levied and the services provided.

Depository and depository participants

When you buy a property, the only way to identify and claim ownership is through property papers. Hence, it is essential to keep these documents safe and secure.

Likewise, when you buy a share (which represents part ownership in a company), the only way to claim ownership is through a share certificate. A share certificate is nothing but a document that establishes you as the owner of shares in a company. Before 1996, share certificates existed in paper form. Post-1996, however, share certificates were converted into digital form. The process of converting paper-based share certificates into digital form is called 'dematerialization', often abbreviated as DEMAT.

Did you know that the Harshad Mehta scam of 1992 played a significant role in accelerating the digitization of share certificates? I'd suggest watching the SonyLIV series on the Harshad Mehta saga—it offers a good perspective of the market ecosystem before it went digital.

Share certificates in DEMAT form need to be stored digitally. The place where these digital certificates are stored is called a DEMAT account. A depository is a financial intermediary that offers DEMAT account services. Think of the DEMAT account as a digital vault for your shares. As I mentioned earlier, your broker's trading account and your DEMAT account are interlinked.

For example, in the earlier Infosys illustration, after you buy 100 shares of Infosys and the transaction is completed, the role of your trading account is done. The shares you purchased are automatically credited to your DEMAT account.

Likewise, when you wish to sell Infosys shares, you log into your trading account and sell the stock. The act of selling happens through your trading account. But at the backend, since your trading and DEMAT accounts are linked, the broker pulls out the shares from your DEMAT account.

At present, only two depositories offer DEMAT account services in India: The NSDL and CDSL. There is virtually no difference between the two, and both operate under strict SEBI regulations.

Just as you cannot walk into the NSE to open a trading account, you cannot walk into a depository (NSDL or CDSL) to open a DEMAT account. To open a DEMAT account, you must go through a depository participant (DP). A DP helps you set up your DEMAT account with a depository and acts as an intermediary between you and the depository. DPs, too, are governed by regulations laid out by SEBI.

Most brokers in India are also DPs. This is why a broker typically offers both trading account and DEMAT account services.

Banks

Banks play a straightforward role in the market ecosystem. They help facilitate fund transfers between your bank account and your trading account. Your trading account and bank account are linked, and brokers set up this linkage after verifying your bank account details.

You can link multiple bank accounts to your trading account, from which you can transfer funds and trade. However, irrespective of how many bank accounts you link to your trading account, funds can be withdrawn to only one bank account. The account you choose for withdrawals (from your trading account) is called the 'primary account'. You can add funds from all linked bank accounts, but withdrawals are processed only to the primary bank account. Most brokers allow you to designate only one bank account as the primary account.

At this stage, you must have realized that three financial intermediaries operate through three different accounts: A trading account offered by your broker, a DEMAT account offered by the depository participant (also your broker) and a bank account offered by a bank. It is the broker's job to ensure these linkages are seamless, giving you a smooth trading and investing experience.

NSE Clearing Limited and ICCL

NSE Clearing Limited and ICCL are wholly owned subsidiaries of the NSE and BSE, respectively.

The job of a clearing corporation is to ensure the settlement of your trades and transactions. For example, if you buy one share of Biocon at ₹365 per share, someone must sell that share to you at ₹365. In other words, money (₹365) has to be exchanged between the buyer and the seller. In a typical transaction like this, the clearing corporation's role is to ensure the following:

- **Match the debit and credit** between the buyer and the seller

- **Ensure there are no defaults:** Once a transaction is executed, neither party should be able to back out, thereby defaulting on the transaction.

For all practical purposes, it's fine not to know much about NSE Clearing Limited or ICCL, simply because you, as a trader or investor, will not interact with these agencies directly. What is important to know is that these institutions are heavily regulated and work towards smooth settlement and efficient clearing.

Clearing corporations are also involved in the margining process, which is critical when trading complex instruments such as futures and options (F&O). Perhaps a topic for another day.

Key takeaways

- The market ecosystem is built by a cluster of financial intermediaries, each offering services essential to market functioning.

- A stockbroker is your gateway to the markets, so choose a broker that matches your requirements.

- A stockbroker provides you with a trading account, which is used for all market-related transactions (buying and selling financial instruments such as shares).

- A depository is a corporate entity that holds shares electronically in your name. Your account with the depository is called a 'DEMAT' account.

- There are only two depositories in India—NSDL and CDSL.

- To open a DEMAT account with a depository, you must liaise with a depository participant, which acts as an intermediary between you and the depository.

CHAPTER 4

The IPO Markets: Part 1

The initial chapters set the context for why you need to invest in equities and the various entities involved in making this investing experience seamless.

At this point, I want you to take a step back and ask yourself a few fundamental questions: Why do companies exist in the stock markets? Why do companies go public and list themselves? What does 'public' mean? What does an IPO mean? What is the difference between a public company and a private company?

A good understanding of these concepts lays a sound foundation for all future topics. In this chapter and the next, we will learn about why companies go public and, in the process, also learn a few important financial concepts.

Origin of a business

To understand why a company files for an IPO and goes public, we need to take a few steps back and begin at the very origins of a typical business. Let me attempt to weave a story to help you understand this better. I'll break this story into several scenes to show how a typical business evolves over time and the circumstances that lead a company to list in the public market.

Scene 1: The angels

Imagine a passionate entrepreneur with a super-simple business idea—to create highly fashionable, organic cotton T-shirts. The designs are unique, something younger folks can relate to; the pricing is spot on; the quality is great; and even the manufacturing process is well thought out. The entrepreneur is confident the business will click and is enthusiastic about getting started.

But at this stage, every entrepreneur faces a typical problem—how to fund the idea. In this case, for example, funds will be required to set up an office, establish a design studio, hire people, set up a small printing unit, procure T-shirts, build inventory, start a marketing channel and so on. Assume the money required to kick-start the idea is ₹5 crore.

Ideas are great, but someone has to put money on the table to encourage the entrepreneur to go ahead and take the risk. Getting that money becomes even more difficult if the entrepreneur has no business background and is trying this out for the first time. At this stage, with no credibility and just a business presentation, the entrepreneur is unlikely to attract serious investors. Chances are that the entrepreneur will approach family and close friends to pitch the idea and raise some money to get the business off the ground.

Let us assume the entrepreneur pools some of their own money and convinces two good friends to invest in the business. Most likely, these two friends invest not because they love the business idea, but because they are friends and genuinely want to help. In this context, the two friends are referred to as angel investors. Please note that angel money—the money given by these two friends—is not a loan but rather an investment in the business.

So let us imagine that the promoter (entrepreneur) and the angels raise ₹5 crore in capital. This initial money, which allows the business to kick-start operations, is called the 'seed fund'. The seed fund is typically led by angels. Sometimes, seed funding is also called a friends and family round, which, as you may have realized, is an apt term in our example.

It is important to note that the seed fund does not sit in the entrepreneur's personal bank account but in the company's bank account.

Angel funding need not always come from friends. There are professional angel investors—typically wealthy individuals—who invest in early-stage companies they believe have potential.

In return for the initial seed investment, the original three (the promoter and the two angels) are issued share certificates of the company, which entitle them to ownership in the business.

Now think about the T-shirt venture at this stage. What does the company really have? Well, apart from a business plan, the only real asset they own is the ₹5 crore in the company's bank account. The business has not yet created any real value. Hence, the value of the company is largely equal to the cash it owns—in this case, ₹5 crore. Of course, one could argue that the company's value is the cash plus the uniqueness of the business idea, and therefore higher than ₹5 crore, but we won't get into that here.

Issuing shares is quite straightforward. The company assumes that each share is worth ₹10, and since there is ₹5 crore in share capital, there would be 50 lakh shares, each with a value of ₹10. In this context, ₹10 is called the face value of the share. The face value could be any number—₹1, ₹5, ₹10 or sometimes even higher. If the face value is ₹5, the number of shares would be 1 crore, and so on.

Backed by the seed fund, the promoter kick-starts business operations. The entrepreneur moves cautiously, hires the right people, establishes the right processes and starts manufacturing high-quality T-shirts.

At this stage, the entrepreneur has a small manufacturing unit and one store to retail the product. The business is now up and running.

Scene 2: The venture capitalist

The entrepreneur's hard work pays off. The T-shirts are selling well, and people are talking about them. Backed by solid sales, the company starts to break even by the end of the first two years of operations. The promoter is no longer a rookie business owner, but is now far more knowledgeable about the business and, of course, more confident. With this newfound confidence, the promoter wants to expand the business by adding another manufacturing unit and a few additional retail stores in the city. The entrepreneur chalks out a plan and realizes that the fresh investment needed for expansion is ₹7 crore.

The entrepreneur is now in a better position compared to two years ago. The big difference is that the business is no longer just a plan, but rather an enterprise that is generating revenues. The healthy inflow of revenue validates both the business and its products.

This means the entrepreneur can now access reasonably savvy investors to invest in the business. In other words, the entrepreneur has moved up the funding ladder.

Although the business is revenue-generating, it is still only two years old—or, in funding terms, an early-stage business. Investors who typically invest at this stage are called venture capitalists (VCs), and the money raised at this point is referred to as Series A funding.

Assume the entrepreneur meets and convinces a VC who agrees to invest the ₹7 crore required to expand the business. Typically, when new capital flows into a business, the following happens:

- There is a dilution of shares by the promoter. Meaning, the promoter will have to part with some of their shares in exchange for the VC's investment.

- The valuation of the business increases. Remember, when the business started, it was valued at ₹5 crore because it had only a business plan and ₹5 crore in the bank. Now, the business is real, with real products and real revenues. So quite obviously, it is more valuable.

- The earlier investors (in this case, the two angels) see notional—or on-paper—profits on their initial investment. At this stage, the promoter and angels have notional wealth. But the VC has just invested money and therefore has not seen any wealth creation yet.

As our story progresses, the promoter now has the capital required to scale the business. As planned, the company sets up an additional manufacturing unit and opens a few more retail outlets in the city. Things are going great; the product's popularity is growing, translating into higher revenues. The management team becomes more professional and operational efficiency increases, leading to better profitability.

Scene 3: The banker

Three more years pass, and the company is now phenomenally successful. It decides to expand further and set up retail shops across three more cities. These are not run-of-the-mill outlets, but experience centres located in the heart of high streets. The company also wants to push online sales. To back these ambitious offline and online expansion plans, it plans to increase production capacity and hire more resources. The expenditure incurred by a company to expand its business is called 'capital expenditure' or simply 'CAPEX'.

The management estimates ₹40 crore towards its CAPEX requirements. How does the company get this money, or, in other words, how does it fund its CAPEX?

There are a few options available to raise the required funds:

- The company has made some profits over the last few years; a part of the CAPEX can be funded using these profits. This is referred to as funding through internal accruals.

- The company can approach another VC and raise an additional round of funding by allotting more shares. This is called 'Series B funding'.

- The company can approach a bank for a loan. Given that the company has been doing well, the bank would be willing to consider this request. This loan is also referred to as 'debt'.

Assume the company exercises all three options to fund its CAPEX. It ploughs back ₹15 crore from internal accruals, plans a Series B by divesting more equity for a consideration of ₹10 crore from another VC, and borrows ₹15 crore from a bank.

Pause for a minute and ask yourself these two questions:

- What happens to the valuation of the business? Remember, we started with a valuation of ₹5 crore.

- Who are the ones seeing notional wealth creation?

I hope you were able to answer these questions comfortably.

With the new VC investing ₹10 crore through the Series B round, the company's valuation increases yet again. With the rise in valuations, the earlier investors tend to make bigger notional profits. These are:

- The promoter
- The two angel investors
- The VC who invested in the Series A round

The latest VC, having just invested in Series B, is yet to see any notional gains.

I would also encourage you to think about the wealth created over the years. This is exactly what happens when entrepreneurs with great business ideas are backed by a highly competent management team.

Real-world examples of such wealth-creation stories include companies such as Infosys, Page Industries, Eicher Motors, Titan Company, Bajaj Finserv and HDFC Bank. Internationally, one can think of Google, Apple, Amazon and many others. The list is long—and keeps getting longer as more successful companies emerge.

Scene 4: Private equity

A few more years pass, and the company's success continues to grow. With the growing success of this eight-year-old business, ambitions swell. The company decides to raise the bar and expand across the country. It also diversifies by manufacturing and retailing fashion accessories, designer cosmetics, perfumes, watches and more.

The CAPEX requirement to fuel this new ambition is now pegged at ₹60 crore. The company does not want to raise money through debt because the interest burden—also called finance charges—eats into the company's profits. For example, if the company generates ₹100 in profit and pays ₹10–₹15 towards finance charges, profitability drops to ₹85–₹90.

Instead, the company decides on Series C funding. As this stage, they cannot approach a typical VC because VC funding is usually better suited for early- to mid-stage companies with relatively smaller funding requirements. When the capital requirement becomes bigger, a private equity (PE) investor comes into the picture. Think of PE as the big brother of VC. Here are a few differences between PE and VC:

- VCs tend to cut smaller cheques, while PE investors typically invest much large amounts.

- VCs invest in early-stage businesses, where the risk of business failure is quite high. PE firms invest at a more mature stage and therefore take on comparatively lower risk.

- PE investors, upon investment, often take a seat on the company's board and oversee the company's functioning.

PE investors are usually quite savvy. They are highly qualified and come with excellent professional backgrounds. They invest large amounts of money and tend to place their representatives on the board of the investee company to ensure the business is steered in the required direction.

Usually, PE investments are made to fund large CAPEX ambitions. Unlike VCs, PE investors do not invest in early-stage businesses; instead, they prefer companies that already have a steady revenue stream and have been operational for a few years. Deploying PE capital and utilizing it for CAPEX requirements takes a few years.

Let us assume that the company raises funds from a PE firm and expands its business.

Scene 5: The IPO

Fast forward three years after the PE investment, and the company has progressed well. It has successfully diversified its product portfolio and now has a presence across all major cities. Revenues are good, profitability is stable and the investors are happy. The promoter, however, does not want to settle for just this.

The promoter now aspires to go international! The company wants its brand to be available across all major international cities, with at least two outlets in each key location worldwide.

The company plans to invest in market research to understand local demographics; invest in people, branding and marketing; put legal frameworks in place to operate outside the country; and increase manufacturing capacity. In addition, it needs to invest in real estate across the world. The CAPEX requirement is massive, but the management and the board are confident of the plan. This time, the funds needed amount to ₹1,500 crore.

The company has a few options to fund this CAPEX requirement:

- Fund CAPEX through internal accruals
- Raise Series D funding from another PE fund
- Raise debt from banks
- Float a bond (another form of raising funds)
- File for an IPO
- Use a combination of the above

For convenience, let us assume the company decides to fund part of the CAPEX through internal accruals and the rest via an IPO. When a company files for an IPO, it must offer its shares to the general public. The public may choose to subscribe to these shares by paying a certain price. Now, because this is the first time the company is offering its shares to the public, the process is called an 'initial public offering'.

We are now at a crucial juncture where a few important questions need to be answered:

- Why did the company decide to file for an IPO? In general, why do companies go public?

- Why didn't the company go public during the Series A, B or C stages?

- What happens to the existing shareholders after the IPO?

- What does the general public look for before subscribing to an IPO?

- How does the IPO process unfold?

- Which financial intermediaries are involved in the IPO market?

- What happens after a company goes public?

In the following chapter, we will address each of these questions plus more, and we will also give you more insights into the IPO market. Hopefully, this chapter has helped you better understand the sequence of events that typically drive a company to raise funds through an IPO.

Key takeaways

- Before understanding why companies go public, it is important to understand the origins of a business.

- People who invest in a business at the pre-revenue stage are called angel investors.

- Angel investors take the maximum risk; financially, they take on as much risk as the promoter.

- The money that angels invest to start a business is called the seed fund.

- Angels typically invest a relatively small amount of capital.

- A company's valuation signifies how much it is worth, based on its assets, liabilities and future growth prospects.

- Face value is simply a denominator that indicates the original value of one share. It is also referred to as the notional value of a share.

- Money spent by a company on business expansion is called capital expenditure, or CAPEX.

- Series A, B and C are funding rounds that a company raises as it grows. In most cases, the later the series, the higher the company's valuation.

- Beyond a certain size, VC funds typically don't invest in a business, and companies seeking larger investments must approach PE firms.

- PE firms invest large sums of money, usually at a more mature stage of the business.

- In terms of risk, PE firms have a lower risk appetite compared to VCs or angels.

- Typical PE investors place their representatives on the investee company's board to ensure the business moves in the right direction.

- A company's valuation increases as and when the business, revenues and profitability increase.

- An IPO is a process through which a company raises funds from the general public. These funds can be used for various purposes—CAPEX, restructuring debt, rewarding shareholders and so on.

The IPO Markets: Part 2

Ihope the previous chapter gave you a perspective on the circumstances that lead a company to go public. I agree that the story was oversimplified, but that was intentional. The idea was to help you broadly understand how a company evolves and matures over time, and how funding needs differ at various stages. More importantly, I hope it helped you understand at what point an IPO becomes a viable funding option for a company.

Understanding the circumstances leading to an IPO is important because the IPO market—also called the primary market—often attracts many first-time stock market investors. India has seen a remarkable share of such IPOs over the decades—from Reliance in the 1980s, to the IT companies' IPOs in the 1990s, to Maruti Suzuki's IPO in 2003, to the latest internet-based companies' IPOs such as Zomato, Nykaa, Paytm and Urban Company.

Given that IPOs have become the gateway for many investors, it's important to understand the technicalities of the primary market. In this chapter, we will explore the IPO process and the various aspects of a company's public offering.

Why do companies go public?

We closed the previous chapter with a few unanswered questions: Why did the company decide to file for an

IPO? Why do companies go public? What happens after the IPO?

One of the most common reasons for a company to file for an IPO is business expansion—what we referred to in the previous chapter as CAPEX requirements. Companies raise money to fuel their business expansion plans, which could include expanding manufacturing facilities, setting up greenfield projects, launching new products: or upgrading machinery.

However, capital expenditure is not the only reason. Companies might have other motivations for raising funds. For instance, if a company has borrowed heavily from banks or other institutions, it can raise money from the public via an IPO and use the proceeds to repay high-interest loans. By doing so, the company reduces its interest charges and increases profitability.

Sometimes, it's a combination of reasons. For example, as I write this, Torrent Gas—a gas distribution company—is preparing to file a ₹3,000-crore IPO. The company has stated that the funds will be used partly to reduce debt and partly to fund CAPEX.

Here's a simple exercise for you: Think of a company that has recently gone public and research the reason for its IPO. It will be interesting to correlate your understanding with an actual IPO.

The promoter gains three key advantages by taking the company public:

- **Raises funds** to address whatever the funding need may be.

- **Avoids additional debt**, which means no finance charges to pay, translating into better profitability.

- **Spreads risk** across a large group of investors instead of relying on one large investor—hundreds or thousands of retail investors are better than one large PE investor.

There are additional advantages to filing for an IPO:

- **Provide an exit for early investors:** Once the company goes public, its shares begin trading on the stock exchange. Existing shareholders—promoters, angel investors, VCs or PE funds—can use this opportunity to sell their shares in the open market and realize returns on their initial investments. Of course, there is typically a lock-in period before early investors can exit, but that's a separate consideration. In our example from the previous chapter, the two angels, the VCs and the PE investor can all exit their investments and convert their notional profits into real profits. Naturally, if they believe their investment will continue to grow, they can hold their positions. It all depends on how they perceive the business's future prospects.

- **Reward employees:** Employees often receive shares as an incentive through arrangements called 'employee stock options' or ESOPs. These shares are typically allotted at a discount. If the company performs well, its valuation increases, share prices rise, and the ESOPs become more valuable, creating wealth for employees. Well-known examples where employees benefited from ESOPs include Google, Infosys, Twitter, Facebook, Amazon, Zomato, Swiggy, Ola and Ather Energy.

- **Improve visibility:** Going public increases visibility as the company becomes publicly held and traded. This generates greater public interest in the company, indirectly helping its growth.

Merchant bankers

Having decided to go public, the company must complete a series of steps to ensure its IPO is successful and attracts investor applications. IPO success is usually measured by the subscription rate—that is, how many shares the company offers versus how many investors subscribe to.

Think of an IPO as a grand Indian wedding—it's like a marriage between the company and its investors. To ensure the wedding goes smoothly, families typically appoint wedding planners who meticulously plan every aspect, from guest lists and decorations to guest management and venue details. Similarly, when a company goes public, it appoints a merchant banker, also called a book running lead manager (BRLM) or simply a lead manager (LM).

The merchant banker's job is to assist the company with various aspects of the IPO process, including:

- **Due diligence:** Conducting comprehensive due diligence on the company filing for an IPO, ensuring full compliance with regulatory requirements laid down by SEBI, and issuing a due diligence certificate

- **Documentation:** Working closely with the company to prepare listing documents, including the draft red herring prospectus (DRHP). The DRHP is a comprehensive document detailing every aspect of the business—from its origins and evolution to inherent business risks and financial statements. If you want to understand a company as well as its promoters do, diving deep into the DRHP is essential. Today, AI tools can help summarize these otherwise 300- to 400-page documents effectively.

- **Underwriting shares:** Underwriting involves the merchant banker agreeing to take up any unsubscribed portion of an IPO. This applies only to fresh shares issued during the IPO. If subscription exceeds a defined threshold but is not fully subscribed, the merchant banker absorbs the remaining shares. If subscription falls below the threshold, the IPO is deemed unsuccessful and all investor money is refunded.

- **Price discovery:** Helping the company arrive at the IPO price band. A price band is the lower and upper limit within which the company sells its shares to IPO applicants. For example, Urban Company's IPO had a price band of ₹98 to ₹103.

- **Marketing:** Assisting with roadshows, which are promotional and marketing activities for the company's IPO.

- **Coordination:** Appointing and coordinating with other intermediaries, including registrars, bankers and advertising agencies, while also developing marketing strategies for the IPO issue.

Once the company partners with the merchant banker, they work together to take the company public.

Sequence of events for an IPO

Every step in the IPO process must comply with SEBI guidelines. Generally, the following sequence applies:

- **Appoint a merchant banker:** For large public issues, companies can appoint multiple merchant bankers.

- **Approach SEBI with a registration statement:** This document contains details about the company's business, why it plans to go public, and its financial health.

- **Receive regulatory approval:** Once SEBI receives the registration statement, it conducts due diligence and confirms whether the company can proceed with the IPO. In some cases, SEBI may request additional documentation for clarity.

- **Prepare the DRHP:** After receiving SEBI's initial approval, the company prepares the DRHP for public circulation. The DRHP typically contains:

  - The estimated size of the IPO

  - The estimated number of shares being offered to the public

  - The purpose of the IPO and how the company plans to utilize the funds, including timelines

  - A business description, including the revenue model and expenditure details

  - Complete financial statements

  - Management discussion and analysis—how the company perceives future business operations

  - Business risks

  - Management details and backgrounds

- **Market the IPO:** This stage resembles a typical marketing campaign with TV advertisements, management interviews and print ads. The purpose is to build awareness about the company and its IPO offering. This activity is called the IPO roadshow.

- **Fix the price band:** The company decides the price range within which it will offer shares to the public. This is a critical aspect of an IPO and often a deciding factor. If the price band is significantly off market, it may adversely impact the IPO's subscription rate. The price band reflects the company's valuation—a very high price band signals high valuation, which may attract fewer investors.

- **Book building:** Once the roadshow concludes and the price band is fixed, the company officially opens the window for public subscription. For example, if the price band is ₹100 to ₹120, the public can bid at any price within this range. Collecting bids at different price points and quantities is referred to as the book-building process. This process helps determine what the public is willing to pay for the issue, also known as price discovery.

- **Closure:** Once the book-building window closes (typically after a few days), the listing price is determined. This price point is usually the level at which the maximum number of bids are received.

- **Listing day:** This is when the company is listed on the stock exchange. Once the stock goes public, it can trade at any price determined by market demand and supply. For instance, Urban Company Limited had a price band of ₹98–₹103, but on listing day, the stock traded at ₹164 per share. Any amount above ₹103—in this case, ₹61—represents listing day gains.

What happens after the IPO?

This entire set of activities—from appointing a merchant banker to conducting roadshows, determining valuation, and completing the book-building process—constitutes primary market activity. The moment a stock is listed and debuts on the stock exchange, it begins trading publicly in the secondary market.

Once the stock transitions from the primary to the secondary market, it trades daily on the stock exchange, with investors regularly buying and selling the listed shares.

Why do people trade? Why does the stock price fluctuate? How does the company benefit from these daily price fluctuations? We will answer all these questions and more in subsequent chapters.

Some key IPO jargon

Before we conclude this chapter, let's review some important IPO terminology:

Under-subscription: If a company offers 1,00,000 shares to the public but receives bids for only 90,000 shares during book-building, the issue is under-subscribed. This indicates negative public sentiment.

Oversubscription: If there are bids for 2,00,000 shares when only 1,00,000 shares are on offer, the issue is oversubscribed by two times (2x).

Green shoe option: A provision in the issue document that allows the issuer to authorize additional shares (typically 15 per cent) for distribution in the event of oversubscription. This is also called the overallotment option.

Fixed-price IPO: Sometimes, companies fix the IPO price rather than opting for a price band. Such issues are called fixed-price IPOs.

Price band and cut-off price: A price band is the range within which investors can bid for the IPO. For example, if the price band is ₹100 to ₹130, bids can be placed within this range. If it lists at ₹125, then ₹125 is referred to as the cut-off price.

Recent IPOs in India

The table below provides a snapshot of some recent IPOs in India. With all the background information you now have, reading this table should be easy.

IPOs in India (2025–26)

No.	Company	Reason for IPO	Price band (₹)	Cut-off price (₹)	Listing day price (₹)
1	Urban Company	Fund technology, cloud infrastructure, office leases and market expansion	98–103	103	164.81
2	Jay Ambe Supermarkets	Store acquisition, retail expansion and working capital	75–78	78	90.25
3	Dev Accelerator	Fund fit-outs for workspaces, debt repayment and CAPEX	56–61	61	61.00
4	Galaxy Medicare	Machinery CAPEX, working capital and general purposes	51–54	54	46.35
5	Shringar House (of Mangalsutra)	Product portfolio, business expansion and working capital for jewellery and accessories	155–165	165	189.62

I hope these last two chapters have given you a clear understanding of why companies file for IPOs and what happens during the IPO process. In the next chapter, we'll focus on understanding secondary markets and the various nuances surrounding them.

Key takeaways

- Companies go public to raise funds, provide exits for early investors, reward employees and gain visibility.

- Merchant bankers act as key partners during the IPO process.

- SEBI regulates the IPO market and has the final authority on whether a company can go public.

- As an IPO investor, you should read the DRHP to understand the company in detail.

- Most IPOs in India follow a book-building process.

CHAPTER 6

Public Limited Company

The two-part IPO chapters helped us understand the IPO process and the circumstances that lead a company to offer its shares to the public and raise funds. To reiterate, when a company files for an IPO, activities such as filing the DRHP, participants applying for an IPO, placing bids, determining the cut-off price and waiting for the stock to list all fall under primary market activities.

Once the stock is listed, we move away from the primary market and enter the secondary market, which is a completely different ball game and where your longer-term wealth-building activity takes place. With this background, I think we are now set to explore the stock markets (the secondary markets, in particular) in greater detail.

Once a company becomes publicly traded, it is obligated to disclose all information related to its business to the public. Think about it: The company is no longer privately held. By raising money from the public, a part of the company now belongs to the public, or in other words, the retail investors. Hence, it becomes necessary and mandatory for the company to distribute information in an orderly fashion so that all investors receive it at the same time.

By now, you also know that the shares of a public limited company are traded daily on stock exchanges such as the NSE and BSE. Share prices move up and down, but have you ever wondered why? Why does a price rise? Why does it suddenly crash? Why are there days when the price does not move? What motivates people to buy and sell? These questions can be endless.

Of course, there are a few reasons why market participants trade stocks and why prices fluctuate. In this chapter, we will explore some of these key reasons.

What is the stock market?

As we discussed in an earlier chapter, the stock market is an electronic marketplace where buyers and sellers express their views to buy and sell.

Let's step away from stock markets for a moment and move to more familiar ground: Our local vegetable markets. Imagine it's 8.30 p.m., the market is about to close and you want to buy onions. Of course, you can open your favourite quick commerce app, tap a few buttons and get them delivered in ten minutes. However, for the sake of learning, let's go back to the good old days of visiting the market, chatting with the vegetable seller, negotiating the price and buying what we need.

The vegetable seller quotes ₹30 per kilo. If you think the price is fair, you buy a kilo of onions and head back home.

Now, imagine this: Overnight, there is news of a farmers' protest, and farmers collectively decide to cut the city's supply of vegetables.

What do you think the price of onions will be the next morning? Will it still be ₹30 per kg? Obviously not. Since the supply of onions has tightened, prices will rise—perhaps to ₹50 or even ₹100 per kilo.

Notice how the price of onions fluctuated overnight. It changed because the news impacted sentiment, which in turn moved the price of onions.

The same thing happens in the stock market. News flow impacts stock prices. One of my favourite examples is the leadership vacuum at Infosys in 2013. I remember this because I was an investor in Infosys at the time and saw the stock price fluctuate heavily.

In late 2013 and early 2014, Infosys faced a management succession issue, with most of the company's senior executives resigning. This leadership vacuum weighed heavily on the company's reputation, and as a result, the stock price dropped from ₹3,500 to ₹3,000.

Now, keeping this in perspective, assume there are two traders—A and B.

Trader A's view on Infosys: Trader A believes the stock price is likely to fall further because the company will find it challenging to find a new CEO. Essentially, A sees this as bad news for the company.

Trader B's view on Infosys: Trader B looks at the same situation very differently. According to her, the leadership vacuum is exaggerated, and a large company like Infosys—with a strong leadership track record—will easily tide over the situation. Trader B is, in fact, optimistic about the future of Infosys.

The stock price of Infosys is ₹3,000, and I have a question for you.

Place yourself in A's shoes. Based on A's point of view, would you want to buy Infosys, or, if you already own the shares, would you want to sell them?

Now place yourself in B's shoes. Based on B's perspective, would you want to buy Infosys, or, if you already own the shares, would you want to sell them?

I hope you arrived at the right answers.

Clearly, A is pessimistic about the future of Infosys and expects the price to go down further. Hence, at ₹3,000 per share, A would prefer to be a seller of Infosys.

B, on the other hand, is optimistic about the company's future. She perhaps thinks that the fall from ₹3,500 to ₹3,000 is an overreaction and hence sees this as an opportunity to buy Infosys.

You see, it's the same stock price and the same company, but the two traders have two different perspectives, and therefore different opinions, leading to different actions in the stock market.

Now, both A and B place orders to buy and sell the stocks through their respective stockbrokers. The stockbrokers route the orders to the stock exchange, which then ensures the two orders are matched and then executes the trade. This is the primary role of the stock market—to facilitate transactions between different market participants.

A stock market is where market participants can trade shares of any publicly listed company based on their individual points of view, as long as there are other participants with an opposing view. After all, it is these differing opinions that make a market.

What moves the stock price?

Let's continue with the Infosys example to understand how stock prices move. Imagine you are tracking Infosys's share price.

It is 10 a.m. Infosys is trading at ₹3,000 per share. The management issues a press release announcing that it has finally appointed a seasoned veteran as the new CEO, thereby putting an end to the leadership vacuum. The new CEO is expected to steer the company to greater heights and work towards a new set of initiatives while maintaining healthy revenue and profitability.

I have two questions for you:

- How will Infosys's stock price react to this news?
- If you were to place a trade in Infosys, what would it be—buy or sell?

The answer to the first question is quite simple. The news is positive, so the stock price will react positively. Infosys had a leadership issue, and the company has now fixed it. When positive announcements are made, market participants tend to buy the stock, often at prevailing prices, which cascades into a stock price rally.

HOW BUYERS MOVE THE MARKETS

No.	Time (a.m.)	Stock price (₹)	Seller's demand (₹)	Buyer's action	New stock price (₹)
1	10.00	3,000	3,002	Buy	3,002
2	10.01	3,002	3,006	Buy	3,006
3	10.03	3,006	3,011	Buy	3,011
4	10.05	3,011	3,016	Buy	3,016

Notice that the buyer is willing to pay whatever price the seller asks—this is when the market is said to be bullish. In a bullish market, buyers tend to overlook business metrics such as valuation and are willing to buy stocks at almost any price, thereby pushing the prices higher.

As you can see, the stock price jumped by ₹16 in a matter of five minutes. Though this is a hypothetical situation, it is realistic in terms of price jumps and investor behaviour in stock markets. Sellers get greedy; they want higher prices. Buyers are fearful of missing out on an opportunity to buy, so they keep buying regardless of price.

In general, stock prices increase when the news is good or is expected to be good.

In this particular case, the stock moves up for two reasons. First, the leadership issue has been fixed. Second, the new CEO is expected to steer the company to greater heights.

The answer to the second question I posed earlier is now quite simple—you would buy Infosys stock because the news is positive.

Now, let's extend this example. Imagine that on the same day, at 12.30 p.m., the National Association of Software and Services Companies (NASSCOM) makes a statement saying that banks and manufacturing companies are likely to cut their IT spending by 15 per cent for the rest of the year. The cut in IT budgets could impact the revenues of the IT industry as a whole.

For those unaware, NASSCOM is a trade association of Indian IT companies.

By 12.30 p.m., let us assume Infosys is trading at ₹3,030. Here are a few questions for you:

- How does this new information impact Infosys?

- With this information, would you buy Infosys or sell it?

- What do you think will happen to other IT stocks in the market?

Before we answer these questions, let's analyse NASSCOM's statement in more detail.

NASSCOM says that IT budgets are likely to shrink by 15 per cent. This implies that IT companies' revenues and profits are likely to decline. The extent of the impact will vary from company to company, depending on factors such as operating efficiency. This is where strong management with a good operating track record comes into play. The management's experience in riding out the headwinds will come in handy.

That said, for the IT industry as a whole, this development is not good news.

Let us now try to answer the questions raised above.

Infosys is a leading IT major in the country and will certainly react to this news. The reaction, however, could be mixed because there was positive news specific to Infosys earlier in the day. That said, a 15 per cent revenue decline is a serious matter, and hence, Infosys stocks are likely to trade lower.

At ₹3,030, if one were to initiate a new trade based on this fresh information, it would likely be a sell on Infosys.

The information released by NASSCOM applies to all IT stocks, not just Infosys. Hence, all IT companies are likely to witness selling pressure.

As you can see, market participants constantly react to news and events. They form opinions and stories about what the future might look like based on the news flow. Opinions differ, and different opinions are what cause the market to move.

At this stage, you may wonder what happens to a company's share price if there is no news at all. Will the stock price remain flat and not move? The answer is yes and no—it depends on the company in question.

For example, assume there is no news related to the following two companies:

- Reliance Industries Limited
- Shree Lakshmi Sugar Mills

Reliance Industries is one of the largest companies in the country. Whether there is news or not, market participants would like to buy or sell its shares, and therefore, the price moves constantly. To what extent will the price move? Well, your guess is as good as mine.

However, in the absence of any news, there are no price triggers; hence, the movement in share price may not be as drastic as it was in the Infosys example.

The second company, Shree Lakshmi Sugar Mills, is relatively unknown and, therefore, may not attract market participants' attention in the absence of news or events. Under such circumstances, the stock price may not move, or move only marginally.

To summarize, stock prices move because of news, events and the opinions and expectations they generate. These events may be specific to a company, an industry, or the economy as a whole. For instance, the rationalization of the goods and services tax (GST) in June 2025 was considered positive for the market, and as a result, the broader stock market moved.

In some cases, even without any news, prices could still move due to the demand-supply dynamics in the market.

How is stock traded?

You have decided to buy 200 shares of Infosys at ₹3,030 and hold them for one year. What is the exact process of buying the stock? What happens after you buy it?

Behind the scenes, systems work seamlessly to ensure your stock market transactions are executed smoothly.

Having decided to buy Infosys, you first log in to your trading account (provided by your stockbroker) and place a buy order. Once you place the order, the following details are validated:

- The price at which you intend to buy Infosys
- The number of shares you intend to buy

Before transmitting this order to the exchange, the broker must ensure that you have sufficient money to buy these shares. If you do, the order is sent to the stock exchange. Once the order hits the exchange, its order-matching algorithm attempts to find a seller willing to sell 200 shares of Infosys at ₹3,030.

The seller could be one person offering to sell all 200 shares at ₹3,030, or it could be ten people selling twenty shares each, or two people selling 1 and 199 shares, respectively. As you can imagine, the permutations are numerous, but in reality, it does not matter much.

From your perspective, all that matters is that you want to buy 200 shares of Infosys at ₹3,030, and you have placed an order to that effect. As long as there are willing sellers in the market, the stock exchange ensures the shares are available to you.

Once the trade is executed, the shares are electronically credited to your DEMAT account and debited from the seller's DEMAT account.

What happens after you buy stock?

After you buy the shares, they are held in your DEMAT account. You are now a part-owner of the company to the extent of your shareholding. To put this in perspective, if you own 200 shares of Infosys, you own 0.000035 per cent of the company.

By owning shares, you are entitled to corporate benefits such as dividends, stock splits, bonuses, rights issues, voting rights and more. We will explore these shareholder privileges at a later stage.

A note on the holding period

The holding period refers to the duration for which you intend to hold a stock. This period can range from a few minutes to a few decades. Legendary investors like Warren Buffett and Charlie Munger have held stocks for multiple decades.

In the example quoted earlier in this chapter, we illustrated how Infosys stock moved from ₹3,000 to ₹3,016 in just five minutes. That's not a bad return for a five-minute holding period! If you are satisfied with it, you can close the trade and move on to find another opportunity. To be clear, this is very much possible in real markets. When things are hot, such moves are quite common. However, the question is: What do you expect and what do you want to achieve?

Yes, a ₹16 move in five minutes seems exciting, but it may not be the safest way to build wealth. In my opinion, for most investors like you and me, wealth creation happens slowly but sustainably over a long period of time.

Regardless of the path you choose for wealth creation, it is important to understand one thing: How to measure returns over your holding period. Doing so helps you develop perspective on what you are doing in the stock market and if you are doing it right.

How to calculate returns

Everything in the markets boils down to one thing: Generating a reasonable rate of return. Returns are usually expressed as annual percentages. There are different kinds of returns you should be aware of. The following will give you a sense of what they are and how to calculate them.

Absolute return: This is the return your trade or investment generates in absolute terms. It helps you answer a simple question: I bought Infosys at ₹3,030 and sold it at ₹3,550. What percentage return did I generate?

The formula to calculate absolute return is:

[Ending Period Value / Starting Period Value – 1] × 100

i.e., [3550/3030 – 1] × 100

= 0.1716 × 100

= 17.16%

A 17.16 per cent return seems like a fantastic return.

Compound annual growth rate: An absolute return can be misleading if you want to compare investment options. Compound annual growth rate (CAGR) helps you answer this question: I bought Infosys at ₹3,030, held the stock for two years, and sold it at ₹3,550. At what annual rate did my investment grow?

CAGR factors in the time component, which we ignored when we computed the absolute return.

The formula to calculate CAGR is:

$$CAGR = \left(\frac{\text{Ending Value}}{\text{Beginning Value}} \right)^{\left(\frac{1}{\#\ of\ years} \right)} - 1$$

Applying this to answer the question:

$$\{[3550/3030]^{\wedge}(1/2) - 1\} \times 100 = 8.2\%$$

This means the investment grew at an annual rate of 8.2 per cent over two years. As of today (2025), the bank fixed deposit market offers returns of around 6.5 per cent with capital protection; hence, an 8.2 per cent return looks just about okay compared to a fixed deposit.

So, always use CAGR to evaluate returns over multiple years. Use absolute return when your time frame is a year or less.

What if you bought Infosys at ₹3,030 and sold it at ₹3,550 within six months? In that case, you have generated 17.16 per cent in six months, which translates to 34.32 per cent (17.16% × 2) for the year.

So, when comparing returns, it's best to express them on an annualized basis.

Where do you fit in?

Each market participant has a unique style of participating in the market. This style evolves as you gain experience and witness market cycles. Your participation style is also defined by the risk you are willing to take in the market. Regardless of how you participate, you can be categorized as either a trader or an investor.

Trader

A trader is someone who spots a market opportunity and initiates a trade with the expectation of exiting profitably at the earliest given opportunity. A trader usually has a short-term view of the markets. They are alert and on their toes during market hours, constantly evaluating opportunities based on risk and reward. There are different types of traders:

- **Day trader:** A day trader initiates and closes positions within the same trading day and does not carry positions overnight. Day traders are generally risk-averse and do not like taking overnight risk. For example: Buy 100 shares of TCS at ₹2,212 at 9.15 a.m. and sell it at ₹2,220 at 3.20 p.m., making a profit of ₹800. A day trader usually trades five to six stocks per day, sometimes even more.

- **Scalper:** A type of day trader. Scalpers usually trade a very large number of shares and hold positions for a short duration to make small but quick profits. For example: Buy 10,000 shares of TCS at ₹2,212 at 9.15 a.m. and sell them at ₹2,212.1 at 9.16 a.m., resulting in a ₹1,000 profit. Scalpers typically execute multiple trades during the day. As you may have noticed, scalpers are highly risk averse.

- **Swing trader:** A swing trader holds positions for a longer duration, typically ranging from a few days to weeks. For example: Buy 100 shares of TCS at ₹2,212 today and sell them at ₹2,300 after a few weeks.

Some successful traders include George Soros, Ed Seykota, Paul Tudor Jones, Michael Steinhardt, Van

K. Tharp, Stanley Druckenmiller and the late Rakesh Jhunjhunwala.

Investor

An investor, on the other hand, is someone who buys a stock expecting significant price appreciation—also called capital appreciation—over the long term. The typical holding period for investors is a few years.

There are two popular types of investors:

- **Growth investors:** The objective here is to identify companies that are expected to grow significantly due to emerging industry and macro trends. A classic example in the Indian context would be buying Hindustan Unilever, Infosys and Gillette India back in the 1990s. These companies witnessed huge growth because of changes in the industry landscape, creating massive wealth for their shareholders.

- **Value investors:** The objective here is to identify good companies, irrespective of whether they are in a growth or mature phase, that are temporarily beaten down due to short-term market sentiment. Such situations can offer opportunities for a great value buy. For example, during the March 2020 Covid crisis, the short-term negative sentiment caused almost all good stocks to fall significantly, only for many of them to post a V-shaped recovery in the subsequent months.

A few successful investors include Charlie Munger, Peter Lynch, Benjamin Graham, Thomas Rowe Price, Warren Buffett, John C. Bogle, John Templeton and Mohnish Pabrai.

So, what kind of market participant would you like to be?

Key takeaways

- A stock market is a place where traders and investors can transact (buy and sell) shares.

- The stock market is an electronic platform where buyers and sellers meet.

- Different opinions make a market.

- Stock exchanges electronically facilitate the transactions between buyers and sellers.

- News and events move stock prices on a daily basis.

- Demand-supply mismatch also causes stock prices to move.

- When you own a stock, you are entitled to corporate benefits such as bonuses, dividends and rights.

- The holding period refers to the duration for which you hold your shares.

- To calculate your rate of return, use absolute returns when the holding period is one year or less. Use CAGR to evaluate growth rate over multiple years.

- Traders and investors differ mainly in their risk appetite and holding periods.

CHAPTER 7

The Stock Market Index

If I were to ask you for a real-time summary of the traffic situation in your city, how would you do it?

Your city may have thousands of main roads, side roads and junctions; it is unlikely that you would check every road in the city to determine the answer. Instead, the wiser thing for you to do would be to quickly check a few important roads and junctions across the city's four directions and observe how traffic is moving. You might then mentally average what you see—if you observe chaotic conditions across these roads, you can conclude the traffic situation is bad; otherwise, you'd say traffic is fairly normal.

Notice how tracking and averaging just a few important roads and junctions helped you summarize the traffic situation of the entire city? These roads effectively act as a barometer for the city's traffic.

Drawing a parallel, if I were to ask you how the stock market is moving today, how would you answer? There are approximately 5,500 listed companies on the BSE and about 2,600 on the NSE. It would be impractical to check every company, figure out if their stock is up or down for the day and then give a detailed answer.

Instead, you would look at a few important companies across key industry sectors. If most of these companies are moving up, you would say the markets are up. If most are down, you would say the markets are down.

And if the trend is mixed, you would say the markets are sideways or flat for the day. The idea is basically to track and average.

Essentially, you are identifying a few companies to represent the broader market. Whenever someone asks you how the markets are doing, you check the general trend of these chosen stocks and answer accordingly. These selected companies, taken together, form the stock market index.

Understanding the index

You may be wondering how you would track these companies individually. By now, you would have understood that each company has its own demand, supply and news flow associated with it, and therefore, each company pursues its own path, just like the traffic situation.

Luckily, you need not track each of these selected companies individually to determine whether they are going up, down or sideways and then average them out. These important companies are already grouped together and continuously monitored to give you this information. This pre-packaged market sentiment indicator is called a 'stock market index'.

There are a few important indices in India. The BSE Sensex represents the Bombay Stock Exchange, and the Nifty 50 represents the NSE. Apart from these two, there are other indices as well, such as the Bank Nifty, Nifty Auto and Nifty IT, which are also quite popular. Bank Nifty represents the banking sector as a whole, Nifty Auto represents the automobile industry and Nifty IT represents the IT industry.

Nifty 50 consists of the most frequently traded stocks on the NSE. We will soon discuss the methodology used to construct these indices. An ideal index provides an up-to-date, accurate representation of market sentiment. Movements in an index reflect the changing expectations of market participants. When an index goes up, it indicates that participants are optimistic about the future. When it drops, it suggests that participants are pessimistic about what lies ahead.

Practical uses of the index

Some of the practical uses of an index are discussed below.

Information: An index reflects the overall sentiment and trend in the market. Broadly speaking, it represents the country's economic outlook. When a stock market index is up, it indicates that people are optimistic about the future. Likewise, when an index is down, it suggests that people are pessimistic about the future.

For example, the Nifty 50 value on 14 October 2025 was 25,191. But around six months before that, the Nifty

50 was at 23,700. The index moved up by 1,500 points, or about 6.3 per cent over six months, indicating bullishness in the market. In other words, market participants were optimistic about India's economic future.

The time frame for observing index movement can be anything. For example, the index at 9.30 a.m. on 13 October 2025 was 25,176, but an hour later, it moved to 25,213—an increase of nearly 37 points within an hour.

Generally speaking, it's better to take a long-term perspective and understand where an index is going and what underlying sentiment is driving it in a particular direction.

Benchmarking: Assume that over the last year, you invested ₹1,00,000 and generated a return of ₹20,000, growing your total investment value to ₹1,20,000. How do you think you performed? Well, on the face of it, a 20 per cent return looks great. But what if I told you that during the same period, the market—say Nifty or the Sensex—moved up by 30 per cent?

Suddenly, it would appear that you underperformed the market! Usually, the objective of market participants is to outperform the index or, at the very least, match what the index offers. Now, if not for a benchmark like an index, it becomes difficult to judge how you performed in the stock market. It's like shooting in the dark. Therefore, an index serves as a reference point to compare and contrast returns.

Trading: Trading on the index is probably one of the most popular uses of an index. The majority of traders in the market prefer to trade indices. They take a broader call on the economy or the general state of affairs and translate that point of view into a trade. The trader usually takes a short-term call on the index.

For example, imagine this situation. At 10.30 a.m., the finance minister is expected to deliver the Union Budget speech. An hour before the announcement, the Nifty index is at 25,000. You expect the budget to be supportive of economic growth.

What do you think will happen to the index? Naturally, the index will move up. So, to trade based on your point of view, you may decide to buy the index at 25,000. After all, the index represents the broader economy.

As per your expectation, the budget turns out to be positive, and the index moves up to 25,500. You can now book your profits and exit the trade with a gain of 500 points!

Trades such as these are executed through what is known as the 'derivatives' segment of the market. But do note that trading in derivatives is highly risky and is advisable only for participants with significant knowledge and experience in the derivatives market.

Portfolio hedging: Investors usually build a portfolio of stocks. A typical portfolio contains fifteen to twenty stocks held for the long term. While these stocks are meant to be held over many years, investors could foresee a prolonged adverse movement in the market—for example, the 2008 subprime crisis and the 2020 Covid crisis—which could erode capital in their portfolio.

In such situations, investors can use the index to hedge their portfolio. Simply put, hedging is a process by which losses in your portfolio are offset by gains from trading the index. By hedging, you are essentially insulating your portfolio from losses.

Of course, a lot depends on your hedging strategy and timing, but at this point, it's enough to be aware that the index plays an important role for investors who want to hedge against a potential downturn in their portfolio.

Index construction methodology

Knowing how an index is constructed is important, especially if one wants to advance as an index trader. As we discussed earlier, an index is a composition of many stocks from different sectors representing the state of the economy. To be included in an index, a stock must meet certain criteria. Once included, the stock should continue to satisfy these criteria. If it fails to do so, it is replaced by another stock that meets the eligibility requirements.

Based on this selection process, the list of constituent stocks is populated. Each stock in the index is then assigned a certain weightage. Weightage, in simpler terms, defines how much influence a certain stock has on the index relative to the other stocks. For example, if ITC Limited has a 3.5 per cent weightage in the Nifty 50 index, it means that 3.5 per cent of Nifty's movement can be attributed to ITC.

The obvious question is: How are weights assigned to the stocks that make up the index?

There are many ways to assign weights, but Indian stock exchanges follow the free-float market capitalization method. Free-float market capitalization is calculated as the product of the number of shares outstanding in the market and the stock price. In simple terms, the number of outstanding shares equal the total of all shares held by the shareholders of a company.

For example, if company ABC has 100 shares outstanding in the market, and the stock price is ₹50, then its free-float market capitalization is:

$100 \times 50 = ₹5,000$

The weights are assigned based on each company's free-float market capitalization. The larger the market capitalization, the higher the stock's weight in the index.

At the time of writing, the following were the top ten index heavyweights on Nifty 50:

TOP 10 NIFTY 50 INDEX SHARES

No.	Company	Sector	Weightage (%)
1	Reliance Industries Limited	Oil and gas	9.21
2	HDFC Bank Limited	Banking	7.43
3	ICICI Bank Limited	Banking	5.82
4	Bharti Airtel Limited	Telecom	5.40
5	TCS Limited	IT	4.86
6	SBI Limited	Banking	4.01
7	Infosys Limited	IT	3.14
8	Bajaj Finance Limited	Financial services	2.86
9	Hindustan Unilever Limited	FMCG	2.52
10	ITC Limited	FMCG	2.49

FMCG: fast-moving consumer goods; IT: information technology

As you can see, Reliance Industries Ltd has the highest weightage. This means the Nifty index is most sensitive to price changes in Reliance.

Sector-specific indices

While the Sensex and Nifty represent the broader market, certain indices represent specific sectors of the economy. These are called sectoral indices. For example, the Bank Nifty on the NSE represents sentiment specific to the banking industry, while the Nifty IT represents the behaviour of IT stocks in the stock market. Both BSE and NSE have sector-specific indices. The construction and maintenance of these indices follow methodologies similar to those used for the broader market indices.

Key takeaways

- An index acts as a barometer of the overall economy.

- An index going up indicates that market participants are optimistic.

- An index going down indicates that market participants are pessimistic.

- There are two main indices in India—the BSE Sensex and NSE's Nifty 50.

- An index can be used for various purposes: Information, benchmarking, trading and hedging.

- Index trading is one of the most popular uses of an index.
- India follows the free-float market capitalization method to construct indices.
- Sector-specific indices convey the sentiment of individual sectors.

CHAPTER 8

Stock Market Jargon

The previous chapters introduced you to stock market jargon, explained in its proper context. Terms like book building, DHRP and CAPEX were explained during the IPO lesson, while index, benchmarking and hedging came up when discussing stock market indices. Learning jargon alongside the relevant concepts helps you understand and relate to them more meaningfully.

However, we've now reached a point where introducing key jargon upfront will help us move forward more smoothly. Let's discuss these essential terms and concepts—they will prove valuable as we explore future topics.

Market sentiment

Bull market (bullish): When you're optimistic about the economic future and expect growth to continue, you're said to be bullish. This applies whether you expect stock prices to rise or anticipate broader market gains. A bull market refers to a period when the stock market index is trending upward. Example: The market was bullish from mid-2020 to early 2022.

Bear market (bearish): When you're pessimistic about the economic future and expect a downturn, you're bearish. If you expect stock prices to decline, you have a bearish outlook. A bear market describes a period when the stock market index is trending downward. Example: The market was bearish from early 2008 to late 2009.

Trend: This refers to the general direction in which a stock or index is moving. If the market is declining rapidly, the trend is bearish. If prices are stuck in a range with minimal movement, the trend is flat or sideways.

Momentum: This measures the rate at which stock prices change. Consider two companies, both with stock prices at ₹100. Company A reaches ₹110 in two days, while Company B takes twenty days to reach the same price. Although both gained 10 per cent, Company A has higher momentum because the rate of change was faster.

Price benchmarks

Face value: The face value (FV), also called par value, indicates the nominal value of a share. This becomes important during corporate actions such as dividends, stock splits or bonuses, which are typically announced relative to the face value. For example, if Infosys has an FV of ₹5 and announces a dividend of ₹63, the dividend yield is 1,260 per cent (63 ÷ 5).

Fifty-two-week high and low: The fifty-two-week high is the highest price at which a stock traded during the past year, while the fifty-two-week low is the lowest. These levels define the stock's trading range over the previous fifty-two weeks. Many traders view a stock reaching its fifty-two-week high as a bullish signal, while hitting a fifty-two-week low suggests bearish sentiment ahead.

All-time high and low: Similar to the fifty-two-week benchmarks, these represent the highest and lowest prices since the stock was first listed. These serve as powerful sentiment indicators, influencing whether the market feels bullish or bearish about a particular stock.

Upper and lower circuit: Stock exchanges impose circuit limits to prevent excessive speculation and wild price swings within short time frames. Based on exchange criteria, circuit limits are set at 2 per cent, 5 per cent, 10 per cent or 20 per cent. For instance, a stock trading at ₹100 with a 10 per cent circuit can move only up to ₹110 (upper circuit) or down to ₹90 (lower circuit) before trading is suspended for a cooling-off period.

Trading positions

Long position: Going long means buying a stock with the expectation that its price will rise. If you've bought, or intend to buy, Biocon shares, you're long on Biocon. Similarly, buying the Nifty index expecting it to trade higher means you have a long position on the Nifty. Bulls typically maintain long positions because they're optimistic about price increases.

Short position: Shorting involves selling a stock you don't own, with the expectation of buying it back later at a lower price. This concept is counterintuitive to most people, so let me illustrate with a story.

Back in mid-2014, when Xiaomi launched the Mi3 smartphone exclusively on Flipkart at an expected price of ₹14,000, my colleague Rajesh missed the registration window. Desperate to get the phone, he offered to buy mine for ₹16,500—even before I purchased it! I accepted the offer and took his money.

I had just sold something I didn't yet own. My only concern was this: What if the phone ended up costing more than ₹16,500? Fortunately, it was priced at ₹14,000. I bought it on Flipkart and delivered it to Rajesh, making a clean profit of ₹2,500.

Notice the sequence: I sold first (at ₹16,500) and bought later (at ₹14,000). This is shorting.

In stock markets, imagine Wipro is trading at ₹260, and you believe the price will drop to ₹240. You can profit from this bearish view by shorting: Sell at ₹260, then buy back at ₹240 when the price falls. Your profit is ₹20, just as if you'd bought at ₹240 and sold at ₹260—but executed in reverse order.

Important notes about shorting

- To hold a short position for multiple days, you need to use F&O.

- Without using F&O, you must close (square off) your short position before the market closes on the same day.

The table below provides a summary of long and short positions:

MARKET POSITION

Position	1st Leg	2nd Leg	Expectation	Profitable when	Loss if
Long	Buy	Sell	Bullish	Stock goes up	Stock price drops
Short	Sell	Buy	Bearish	Stock goes down	Stock price goes up

Square off: This means closing an existing position. If you're long on a stock, squaring off means selling it—you're not taking a short position, you're simply closing your long position. If you're short, squaring off means buying the stock back—you're not going long, you're closing your short position.

When you are	To square off, means
Long	Sell the stock
Short	Buy the stock

This may seem confusing now, but once you execute these transactions in real life, it becomes instantly clear.

Intraday position: This is a trading position you open and close within the same day. All short positions in stocks (when not using derivatives) are intraday positions. I must mention that intraday trading is highly risky and can be addictive. If you're new to the stock market, I strongly advise approaching it with a long-term perspective instead.

Price and volume data

OHLC: This acronym represents key daily price points:

- **O** = Opening stock price
- **H** = Highest price reached during the day
- **L** = Lowest price reached during the day
- **C** = Closing price

Volume: Volume represents the total number of shares traded (both bought and sold) for a particular stock on a given day. For example, on 27 October 2025, Urban Company Limited recorded a volume of 82 lakh shares.

Both OHLC and volume play crucial roles in technical analysis—a method of analysing markets through charts, price movements and volume patterns to make trading decisions.

Market segments

The exchange operates three main segments, each characterized by different risk and reward parameters.

Capital market: This segment offers tradable securities such as stocks and ETFs. When you buy or sell company shares, you're operating in the capital market segment. Intraday stock shorting also falls under this segment. It is sometimes referred to as the spot market or cash market.

Futures and options: Also known as the equity derivatives segment, this is where leveraged products are traded. Index trading, which we discussed earlier, primarily takes place through F&O in this segment.

Wholesale debt market: This segment deals with fixed-income securities, including government securities, treasury bills, bonds issued by public sector undertakings, corporate bonds and corporate debentures.

These are the essential terms you will need going forward. While many more exist, these provide a solid foundation for understanding the concepts we will be exploring in the coming chapters.

CHAPTER 9

Trading Terminal

Over the last several chapters, we have gained an understanding of several key concepts related to the stock market. It is now time to look at how one can actually buy and sell in the market. There are four common ways to place a transaction:

Call and trade: This is the age-old method of transacting in the markets. You pick up your phone, call your stockbroker and request to buy or sell a stock. This requires you to identify yourself with a secure PIN. Until the advent of online trading, call and trade was the default choice for many. Today, however, the number of people opting for this facility is on the decline.

Web application: This is a very popular method to transact in the market. You log in to your broker's web application and place orders electronically. We will focus on this method in this book.

Mobile application: An increasingly popular method is using a broker's mobile application (Android or iOS). These applications are becoming more and more sophisticated, and today you can transact in stocks of any value by swiping left or right on your phone.

Application programming interfaces: Many brokers now offer application programming interfaces (APIs) to developers. Think of an API like a waiter in a restaurant. You (the developer) tell the waiter what you want, the waiter takes your request to the kitchen (the broker's system) and brings back what you asked for—whether that's market data, placing a trade or checking your account balance. Using these APIs, developers can programmatically access the markets. The advantage of APIs is that you can control the look and feel of your trading application. For example, you can run a program to fetch the P&L of your portfolio every 5 minutes.

Regardless of which method you choose, it gives you access to the stock market. Think of this access as a gateway. This gateway allows you to do multiple things, such as transact in stocks, track your P&L, monitor market movements, manage your funds, view stock charts and access trading tools.

This chapter aims to familiarize you with this gateway, also called a 'trading terminal'. To explain the concepts in this chapter, I'll be using Zerodha's trading terminal, called 'Kite'. If you are with another broker, then the trading terminal provided to you will (or should) have similar features and functionality.

You can access the trading terminal by entering the broker-provided URL in your browser. For Zerodha Kite, the URL is kite.zerodha.com. To access the trading terminal, you must have a trading account with your broker. A good trading terminal offers several features, and we'll start by understanding a few basic ones.

I think it makes sense to set ourselves two simple tasks that we will complete using a trading terminal. While doing so, we will learn how the trading terminal works in a practical way. These two tasks are:

- Buy one share of ITC
- Track the price of Infosys

While we complete these tasks, we will also learn the relevant concepts along the way.

The login process

The trading terminal is a sensitive system, as it contains information about your investments in stocks and mutual funds. SEBI, India's market regulator, has been advocating best practices to safeguard trading and investing accounts. After all, many people have their life savings locked in these accounts, so it makes absolute sense to protect them against potential misuse or cyber fraud.

It is the broker's responsibility to ensure they provide adequate security to secure the login process for a trader or an investor. This involves entering your broker-provided user ID (referred to as the Kite ID in Zerodha) and password.

Once you click Login, the user ID and password are authenticated, after which you are prompted to enter a time-based one-time password (TOTP). As the name suggests, TOTPs are time-sensitive and change once every few seconds. This additional layer further enhances account security.

TOTPs can be set up using third-party authentication software such as Google Authenticator or Authy.

LOGIN WITH 2FA

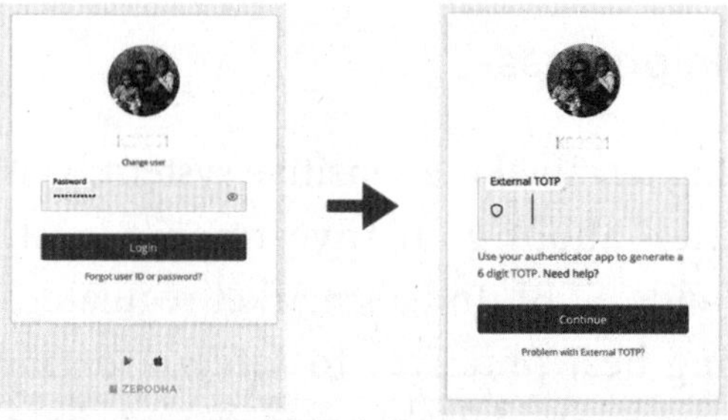

Once you validate the TOTP, you gain immediate access to your trading account.

Market Watch

Once you successfully log in to the platform, you must first populate the 'Market Watch' with the stocks you are interested in. Think of the Market Watch as a blank slate.

Once the stock is added, you can easily transact in it and query information about it.

DASHBOARD

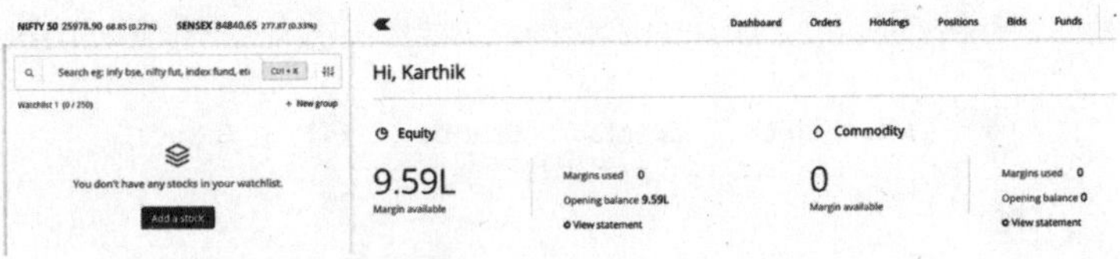

As you can see, there are two sections here. On the left is the blank Market Watch with an option to add stocks. Using the search bar, I can look up any stock I'm interested in, whether I want to buy it, sell it or simply track its movements. On the right side are my fund balances. For now, I have ₹9.6L in my account, which I can use to buy stocks.

You can add funds from your bank account to the trading account or withdraw funds from the trading account to your bank account by clicking on 'Funds', the first option you see at the top right.

Now, let's move on to the first task—buying one share of ITC Limited. As a first step, we need to add ITC to the Market Watch. To do this, search for ITC in the search bar. You'll then see the option to select ITC from different exchanges (NSE or BSE). You can choose either exchange—or both, as long as the stock is listed on both exchanges. If not, it will appear only on the exchange it is listed on.

SEARCH FOR A STOCK

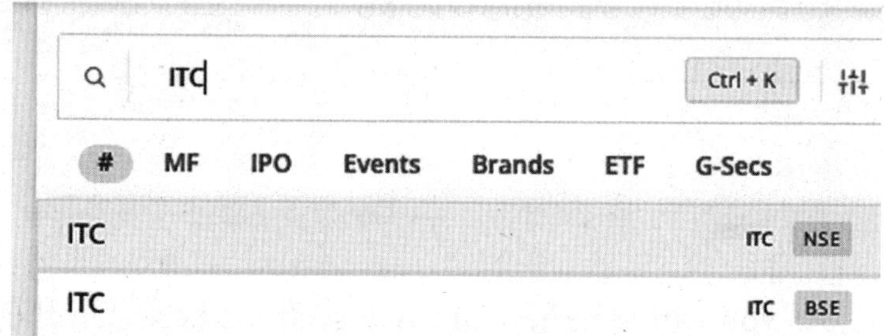

Since we are interested in buying one share of ITC, we select the relevant instrument—ITC Limited—and click on 'Add symbol' to add it to the Market Watch.

MARKET WATCH

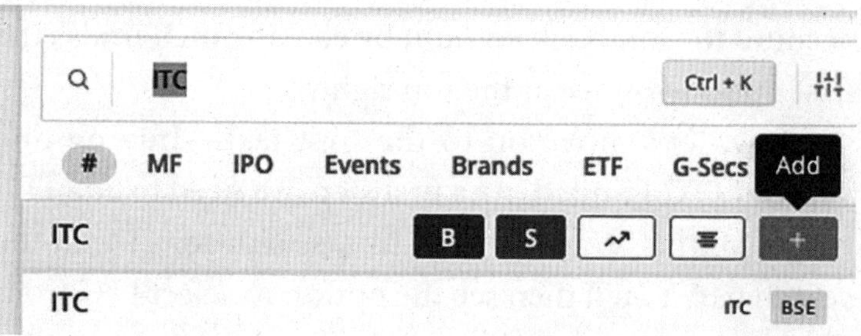

After adding the stock, this is how the stock appears on the Market Watch:

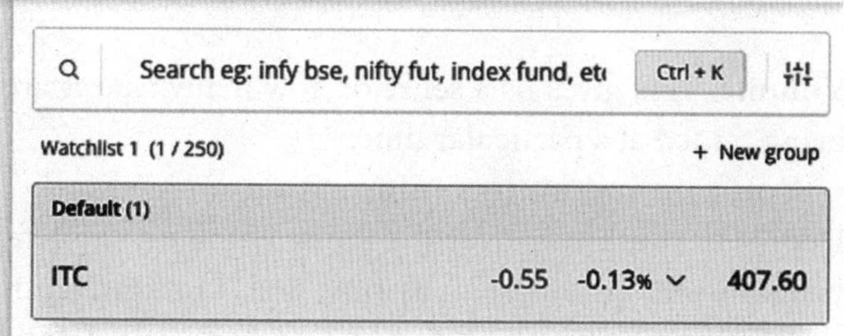

The Market Watch displays the rupee change from the previous day, the percentage change and the last traded price (LTP) of the stock. The LTP provides us with the per-share price of the stock at that exact moment.

In ITC's case, the stock price has declined ₹0.55 from the previous day, which in percentage terms is 0.13 per cent, and the current stock price is ₹407.6.

At this point, we will also need some basic information:

The previous day's close: As the name suggests, this is the stock's closing price from the previous trading day. It helps us understand where the stock price closed yesterday and, with reference to that, at what price it is available today at the time of buying.

OHLC: Open, high, low and close together give us the full picture of the price range within which the stock is trading during the day. Please recall that we discussed OHLC in the previous chapter.

Volume: This gives us a sense of how many shares are being traded at a particular time.

You can find all this information under Market Depth. If you hover over the stock name on the left, you will see options such as Buy, Sell, Market Depth and Chart. Clicking on Market Depth reveals details such as the previous day's close, OHLC, volume and other information, including the best bid and offer price ladder. We will cover the bid and offer prices soon.

MARKET DEPTH

NIFTY 50 26012.90 102.85 (0.40%)　　SENSEX 84949.18 386.40 (0.46%)

Q　Search eg: infy bse, nifty fut, index fund, et｜　Ctrl + K

Watchlist 1　(1 / 250)　　+ New group

Default (1)

ITC　　-0.55　-0.13% ⌄　407.60

Bid	Orders	Qty.	Offer	Orders	Qty.
407.60	5	2677	407.75	2	568
407.55	3	1266	407.80	11	2550
407.50	15	2596	407.85	16	2734
407.45	18	9550	407.90	18	3839
407.40	30	9339	407.95	23	5521
Total		13,54,086	Total		14,19,446

Open	409.75	Prev. Close	408.15
Low	406.45	High	412.00

Volume	50,24,059	Avg. price	407.72
Lower circuit	367.35	Upper circuit	448.95
LTQ	10	LTT	2025-11-17 14:12:21

As you can see, the last traded price of ITC is ₹407.6, and it is trading 0.13 per cent lower than the previous day's close of ₹408.15. The opening price for the day was ₹409.75, which also turned out to be the highest price for the day. The lowest price at which the stock traded during the day was ₹406.45. The volume for the day is close to 50.24 lakh shares.

Buying stock through the trading terminal

Our goal is to buy one share of ITC. Since ITC in now added to our trading terminal, the next step is to invoke a buy order form.

BUY/SELL FROM MARKET WATCH

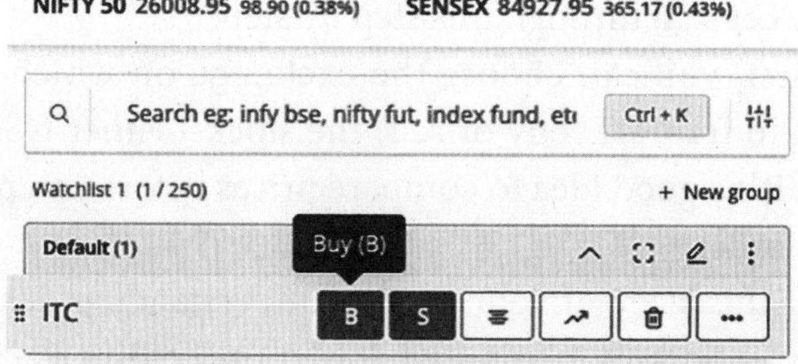

To do this, hover over the stock you want to buy and click on the Buy icon (B). This will bring up the buy order form, as seen below.

BUY ORDER FORM

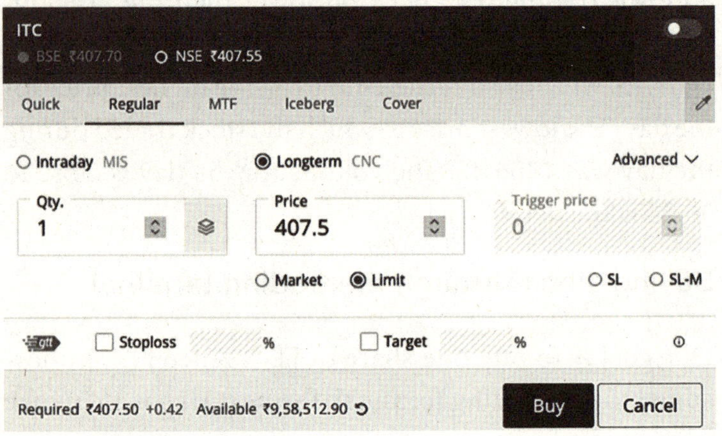

At first glance, the order form may look intimidating, but that's only until you understand what's going on here. Let's go through this step by step.

First, you can choose the exchange on which you want to transact (buy or sell) the stock—either NSE or BSE. It's a good idea to compare prices before you place your order.

At this stage of your market understanding, it's not really important to know what Margin Trading Facility, Iceberg or Cover Order are, so let's skip those for now. You can explore them later when you gain more experience with trading and investing in the market.

There are two options for the duration of the trade:

- Margin intraday square-off (MIS), more commonly called 'intraday'
- Cash and carry (CNC), for long-term investment

Intraday is for active traders who want to buy and sell stocks within the same day, while long-term is for investors who want to hold their stocks in their DEMAT account for a longer period.

Right below the duration, you'll find the quantity and price fields. This part is fairly self-explanatory: quantity is the number of shares you want to buy or sell, while price is the price at which you want to transact.

There are a few more options here, and it's important to understand what each of these means:

- Limit order
- Market order
- Stop-loss order
- Stop-loss market

You can opt for a limit order when you are particular about the price you want to pay for a stock. In our case, the last traded price of ITC is ₹407.6. Say we want to limit our buy price to ₹407.45, fifteen paisa lower than the LTP. In such a situation, you can use the limit feature and specify the price at which you want to buy the stock. The limit feature is great as it gives you control over the price at which you want to buy. However, on the flip side, if the stock price does not fall to your limit price—₹407.45—your order will not be executed and you won't get the shares. This is one of the drawbacks of a limit order. The limit order remains valid until the market closes at 3.30 p.m., after which it gets cancelled.

You can also opt for a market order when you intend to buy at the prevailing market price instead of a specific price. If you place a market order, as long as sellers are available, your order will go through, and ITC will be bought at or around ₹407.6. However, if the price goes up to ₹410 at the moment your market order is placed, then you will end up buying the ITC stock at ₹410.

When you place a market order, you are never entirely sure of the exact price at which the transaction will occur. This uncertainty could be quite risky if you are an active trader. A market order will ensure that your order is always executed, unlike a limit order. Of course, this is assuming there is sufficient liquidity in the market.

Think of it this way: You want to buy a kilo of onions. You go to the nearest vegetable shop and ask the price. If the shopkeeper says ₹50 per kg and you agree to pay that price, that's similar to placing a market order—you pay the price quoted.

On the other hand, if you bargain with the shopkeeper and say you won't pay more than ₹45 per kilo, that's like placing a limit order. Your 'order' will go through only at ₹45, and only if the seller (shopkeeper) agrees to sell at that price.

A stop-loss order protects you from adverse movement in the market after you initiate a position. Suppose you buy ITC at ₹407 with an expectation that the stock will hit ₹415 shortly. But what if the price starts moving down instead? You can protect your position by defining the maximum loss you are willing to take.

For instance, in this example, let's assume you don't want to incur a loss beyond ₹404. This means you have gone long on ITC at ₹407, and the maximum loss you are willing to take on this trade is ₹3 (₹407 – ₹404). If the stock price drops to ₹404, the stop-loss order gets activated, hits the exchange, and you exit the loss-making position. If the price is above ₹404, the stop-loss order stays dormant.

A stop-loss order is a passive order. To activate it, you must enter a trigger price. The trigger price, usually above the stop-loss price, acts as a threshold—only after the stock crosses this price does the stop-loss order transition from a passive order to an active order.

Continuing with our example:

You are long at ₹407. If the trade goes against you, you want to get rid of the position at ₹404. Therefore, ₹404 is the stop-loss price. The trigger price must be equal to or higher than ₹404, say ₹404.5. If the price drops below ₹404.5, the stop-loss order is activated.

Returning to the main buy order form, once the order type is selected, you move to the quantity field. Since the task is to buy one share of ITC, you enter '1' in the quantity box. For now, you can ignore the trigger price and disclosed quantity. The next option to select is the product type.

Select CNC (long-term) for delivery trades. A delivery trade is one where you want to hold the position for at least one day or longer. If you intend to buy and hold the shares for multiple days, months or years, you must ensure the shares reside in your DEMAT account. Selecting CNC is how you communicate this intent to your broker.

Select MIS if you want to trade intraday. In an intraday trade, you buy and sell (or sell and buy) within the same day.

Once these details are filled in on the order form, the order is ready to hit the market. As soon as you click the Submit button, the order is transmitted to the exchange, and a unique order ticket number is generated for your trade.

Once the order is sent to the exchange, it will not be executed unless the price hits the price you have specified—in this case, ₹407.5. As soon as the price drops to ₹407.5 (assuming sellers are willing to sell one share), your order goes through and is executed. At that point, you will own one share of ITC.

In my case, the price dropped at the time of executing the trade, and I ended up buying one share of ITC at ₹406.9.

The order book and trade book

The order book and trade book are like online registers within the trading terminal. The order book keeps track of all the orders you have sent to the exchange, while the trade book tracks all the trades. Think of it this way: When you order goods on Amazon, you first add items to the cart. The cart is like the order book. You can add items, delete them or modify the order from the cart (order book). But once you press the buy button on Amazon, the order is placed and a receipt is generated. The trade book is that receipt. You also receive a detailed receipt via email called a 'contract note', which we will discuss later. For now, think of the trade book as a general receipt for all the trades you carry out on the terminal.

There is a small nuance you should be aware of here. If your order is a limit order, you can add, modify or edit it from the order form. However, if you place a market order, it is executed immediately, leaving no opportunity to modify it.

You can access the order book by clicking the Orders tab.

ORDER PAGE

				Dashboard	Orders	Holdings	Positions	Bids	Funds		
Orders	GTT	Baskets	SIP	Alerts							

Executed orders (1)   Q Search   🖹 Contract note   ↻ View history   ↓ Download

Time	Type	Instrument	Product	Qty.	Avg. price	Status
14:28:26	BUY	ITC NSE	CNC	1 / 1	406.90	COMPLETE

Trades ∧ (1)   Q Search   ↻ View history   ↓ Download

Trade ID	Fill time	Type	Instrument	Product	Qty.	Avg. Price
208525808	14:28:26	BUY	ITC NSE	CNC	1	406.9

The order book provides details of all the orders you have placed. You should access the order book to:

- Double-check order details such as quantity, price, order type and product type

- Note the exact time at which the order was placed

- Modify the orders

- Check status: After placing an order, you can track its status. An order is marked 'open' if it is partially completed, 'completed' if it has been fully executed and 'rejected' if the order was rejected. In case of rejection, the order book also displays the reason.

As you can see, the order to buy ITC has been completed.

Once the order is processed and the trade is executed, the trade details will be available in the trade book. You can find the trade book just below the order book.

Here is a snapshot of the trade book:

Trades ∧ (1)					Q Search	⟳ View history ↓ Download
Trade ID	Fill time	Type	Instrument	Product	Qty.	Avg. Price
208525808	14:28:26	BUY	ITC NSE	CNC	1	406.9

The trade book confirms that the order to buy one share of ITC was executed at ₹406.9. You'll also notice that a unique trade ID number has been generated for the trade.

With this, our first task is complete!

We now officially own one share of ITC. This share will reside in our DEMAT account until we decide to sell it.

The next task is to track the price of Infosys. The first step is to add Infosys to the Market Watch. We can do this by searching for Infosys in the search box.

SEARCH FOR A STOCK

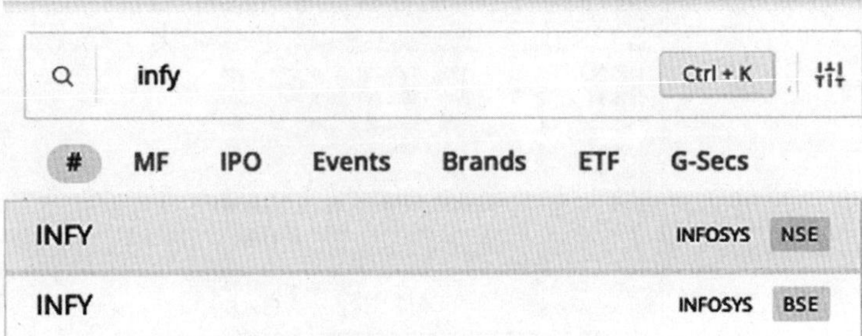

Once we select Infy, we press 'Add' to include it in the Market Watch.

MARKET WATCH

NIFTY 50 25991.15 81.10 (0.31%)   **SENSEX** 84881.35 318.57 (0.38%)

Q	Search eg: infy bse, nifty fut, index fund, etc	Ctrl + K	

Watchlist 1 (2 / 250)   + New group

Default (2)			
ITC	-1.45	-0.36% ˅	406.70
INFY	2.60	0.17% ˄	1505.40

Notice that we now have two stocks on the watchlist—Infy and ITC.

We can now track live price information for Infosys. The last traded price is ₹1,506.2; the stock is up 0.23 per cent. We can now open Market Depth for more information about the stock price.

MARKET DEPTH

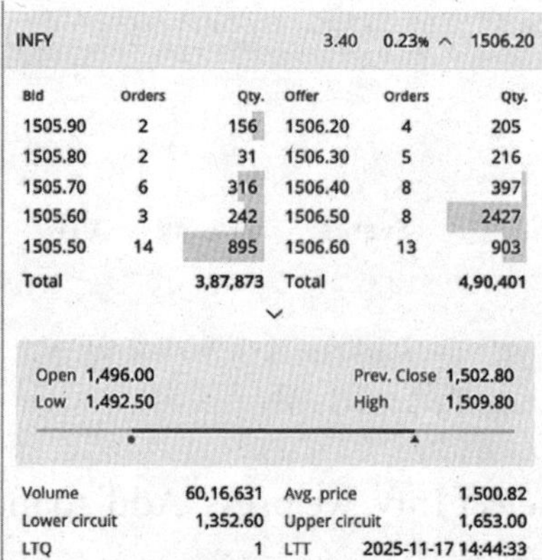

INFY			3.40	0.23% ˄	1506.20
Bid	**Orders**	**Qty.**	**Offer**	**Orders**	**Qty.**
1505.90	2	156	1506.20	4	205
1505.80	2	31	1506.30	5	216
1505.70	6	316	1506.40	8	397
1505.60	3	242	1506.50	8	2427
1505.50	14	895	1506.60	13	903
Total		3,87,873	Total		4,90,401

Open	1,496.00	Prev. Close	1,502.80
Low	1,492.50	High	1,509.80

Volume	60,16,631	Avg. price	1,500.82
Lower circuit	1,352.60	Upper circuit	1,653.00
LTQ	1	LTT	2025-11-17 14:44:33

From the previous day's close of ₹1,502.82, Infosys opened at ₹1,496, making a low of ₹1,492.5 and a high of ₹1,509.8. The trading volume for the day was sixty lakh shares.

Please note that while the opening price remains fixed at ₹1,496, the high and low prices change as and when the price of Infosys changes. For example, if Infosys moves from ₹1,506.2 to ₹1,512, the high price will update to ₹1,512.

MARKET WATCH

NIFTY 50 25991.15 81.10 (0.31%)   **SENSEX** 84881.35 318.57 (0.38%)

Q Search eg: infy bse, nifty fut, index fund, etc	Ctrl + K	₊₊₊

Watchlist 1 (2 / 250)   + New group

Default (2)			
ITC	-1.45	-0.36% ∨	406.70
INFY	2.60	0.17% ∧	1505.40

Besides basic information such as LTP, OHLC and volume, we can dig deeper to understand real-time market participation using Market Depth. I would like to draw your attention to the blue and red numbers, referred to as the bid and offer prices.

Bid and offer prices

If you want to buy a share, you need to buy it from a seller. The seller offers the share at a price they think is fair. This price is called the 'offer price'. In the Market Watch, offer prices are highlighted in red.

Let's analyse this in a bit more detail with an example.

No.	Offer price (₹)	Offer quantity	No. of sellers
1	3,294.80	2	2
2	3,294.85	4	2
3	3,295.00	8	2
4	3,296.20	25	1
5	3,296.25	5	1

By default, the Market Depth window displays the top five bids and offer prices. In the table above, we have the top five offer prices.

The first offer price is ₹3,294.80. At this moment, this is the best price to buy the stock. Only two shares are available at this price, offered by two different sellers (each selling one share).

The next best offer price is ₹3,294.85, at which four shares are available from two sellers. The third best price is ₹3,295, where eight shares are available, offered by two sellers, and so on.

As you can see, the higher the offer price, the lower its priority. For example, the fifth offer price is ₹3,296.25 for five shares. This is because stock exchanges prioritize sellers who are willing to sell their shares at the lowest possible price.

Notice that even if you want to buy ten shares at ₹3,294.8, that won't be possible because only two shares are available at that price. However, if you are not particular about the price (i.e., limit price), you can place a market order. When you place a market order to buy ten shares, this is how it will be executed:

- Two shares bought at ₹3,294.80

- Four shares bought at ₹3,294.85

- Four shares bought at ₹3,295.00

The ten shares are bought at three different prices. Also, in the process, the LTP of this stock will jump up from ₹3,294.8 to ₹3,295. The ten shares are bought at three different prices, and as result the last traded price readjusts and jumps from 3294.8 to 3295.

Now, let's examine bids and what they entail.

If you want to sell a share, you need a buyer who is willing to buy it from you. The buyer will purchase the shares at a price they consider fair. The price a buyer is willing to pay is called the 'bid price'. In the Market Depth window, the bid price is highlighted in blue.

Let's analyse this part in a little more detail.

No.	Bid price (₹)	Bid quantity	No. of buyers
1	3294.75	10	5
2	3294.20	6	1
3	3294.15	1	1
4	3293.85	6	1
5	3293.75	125	1

By default, the Market Depth window displays the top five bid prices. Notice that the best price at which you can sell shares is ₹3,294.75. At this price, you can only sell ten shares, as only five buyers are willing to buy ten shares at that level.

If you were to sell twenty shares at the market price, the execution would occur as follows:

- Ten shares sold at ₹3,294.75

- Six shares sold at ₹3,294.20

- One share sold at ₹3,294.15

- Three shares sold at ₹3,293.85

In a nutshell, bid and offer prices give you information about the top five prices at which buyers and sellers are stacked. You need to understand how buyers and sellers place their trades, especially if you are an intraday trader.

By default, the bid and offer prices are shown only for the top five prices. However, you can gain an insight into the top twenty bids and offers by looking at the twenty-depth window.

Conclusion

The trading terminal is your gateway to the markets and offers a wide range of features useful to traders and investors. At this stage, you should know how to set up a market watch, transact (buy and sell) in stocks, view the order and trade book and understand the market depth window.

One final point before we wrap up this chapter: Trading terminals are continually evolving to improve the user experience (UX). While the UI and UX may change over time, the underlying concepts, such as the order book, trade book, stop-loss orders and limit orders, remain the same.

Key takeaways

- To participate smoothly in the stock market, you must understand how to operate a trading terminal.

- You can load the stocks you are interested in on the Market Watch to track all relevant information.

- The Market Watch displays key data such as LTP, percentage change, OHLC and volumes.

- To buy a stock, invoke a buy order form by pressing the 'B' key; to sell, invoke the sell order form by pressing the 'S' key.

- Choose a limit order when you want to transact at a particular price; otherwise, you can opt for a market order.

- Select CNC as the product type if you want to buy and hold stock across multiple days. Select MIS for intraday trades.

- The order book helps you track open and completed orders. You can modify open orders by clicking on the 'Modify' button at the bottom of the order book.

- Once an order is completed, you can view the trade details in the trade book.

- The Market Watch enables you to see bids and offer prices.

- Bid and offer prices refer to the prices at which you can buy and sell shares. The top five bid and offer prices are displayed in the Market Depth window.

Clearing and Settlement

When you buy a stock, several things happen in the background. Funds are debited from your trading account and credited to the seller's trading account, while the shares are debited from the seller's DEMAT account and credited to your DEMAT account.

While this may seem straightforward, several institutions are involved in ensuring that the transaction is smooth and default-free. The sequence in which these activities are carried out is super important to understand. Broadly speaking, this entire process is called the 'clearing and settlement' of funds and securities.

For instance, when you buy 100 shares of Marico, you need to clearly understand when exactly the money is withdrawn from your trading account and at what point you become entitled to receive the 100 shares. Likewise, when you sell 100 shares of Marico from your DEMAT account, you should know when the shares are debited from your account and when the sale proceeds are credited to you.

A lack of clarity around the clearing and settlement process can leave gaps in one's understanding of market structure and result in several unanswered questions. For this reason, we will explore what happens behind the scenes from the moment you hit that buy button on your trading terminal to the point when the shares are actually credited to your trading account.

We will keep this discussion practical, with a clear emphasis on what you, as an end customer, need to know about clearing and settlement.

What happens when you buy a stock?

Day 1: The trade (T day, Monday)

Assume that on a Monday, you buy 100 shares of company ABC Industries at ₹1,000 per share. The total buy value is ₹1,00,000 (100 * 1,000). The day on which you make the transaction is called the 'trade date', commonly referred to by brokers as 'T day'.

The assumption is that you intend to hold ABC Industries in your DEMAT account for a few days or even years, meaning this is not an intraday trade.

When you place a buy order, the broker quickly validates whether you have the necessary funds in your trading account. In this example, the order will go through only if you have ₹1,00,000 available; otherwise, the order will be rejected.

Assuming the trade is executed through a new-age broker (equity brokerage being zero), the applicable charges are as follows:

No.	Chargeable item	Charges	Amount (₹)
1	Brokerage	0	0
2	Security transaction charges (STT)	0.1% of the turnover	100.00
3	Exchange transaction charges	0.00297% of the order value	2.97
4	SEBI charges	Rs 10 per crore of transaction	0.10
5	GST	18% of brokerage + transaction charges + SEBI charges	0.55
6	Stamp duty	0.015% or ₹1500 per crore on the buy side	15.00
Total			118.62

Please note that these charges are subject to change as the markets evolve and new regulatory changes take effect. You can always consult with your broker to understand the various charges and determine the exact applicable rate when you are ready to carry out a transaction.

In this case, to buy ABC Industries, you must have ₹1,00,000 plus ₹118.62, totalling ₹1,00,118.62, in your trading account. Without the required funds, the order will not be processed and will be rejected.

Assuming the funds are available, the amount is instantly blocked when you place the buy order. However, the shares are not credited to your DEMAT account on T day.

Additionally, on T day, the broker generates a contract note and emails it to your registered email address. A contract note is similar to a bill, detailing all transactions executed during the day. It includes the trade reference number and a breakup of charges levied by the broker. You should save the contract note for future reference and record-keeping.

Day 2: Trade day + 1 (T+1 day, Tuesday)

Starting January 2023, India became the first country to implement a T+1 settlement for all scrips listed on the stock exchanges. This means that if a trade is executed on a Monday (T day), the shares are credited to your DEMAT account the very next day—Tuesday (T+1 day).

On Day 2, also referred to as T+1, the settlement is due to the exchange. Assuming the purchaser and seller are trading through two different brokers, the clearing corporation debits the funds from the buyer's broker's pool account and credits them to the seller's broker's pool account. Think of a pool account as a common account in which shares (or funds) belonging to all the broker's clients are brought forward. It is the broker's responsibility to ensure the necessary funds or shares are further routed from the general pool account to the respective individual client accounts. Also, on T+1 day, the shares will reflect in the purchaser's DEMAT account, indicating that they own 100 shares of ABC Industries.

Before January 2023, India followed a T+2 settlement cycle. For example, if you bought shares on a Monday, they were credited to your DEMAT account only on Wednesday.

Over the years, India has undergone major reforms in the settlement process. You may find it interesting that the Harshad Mehta scam of 1992 triggered these reforms. At that time, settlements followed a T+14 cycle, and shares were delivered in physical form via paper share certificates.

From Harshad Mehta's days to today's T+1 settlement, Indian regulators have played a pivotal role in shaping India's market infrastructure, significantly improving the ease and efficiency of stock market transactions.

What happens when you sell a stock?

The day you sell your shares is again referred to as the 'T day'. When you place a sell order, the shares in your DEMAT account are blocked, and by the end of the day, they are 'earmarked' for settlement. Please refer to the next section to learn more about earmarking.

Before the T+1 day, the earmarked shares are delivered to the depository. On settlement day, the blocked shares are debited from your DEMAT account and transferred to the clearing corporation. Against this debit, you receive a credit for the sale after deducting all charges.

What transpires between T day and T+1 involves a complex settlement process that includes the stockbroker, clearing corporation, depository and stock exchange. Each entity uploads and receives multiple files to ensure the transaction goes smoothly.

As far as you are concerned, what you need to remember is that equity transactions are settled on a T+1 basis. This means that if you are a buyer, the shares are credited to your DEMAT account on T+1, and if you are a seller, the funds are credited to your account on T+1.

What is earmarking?

Earlier, to settle a sell trade, the broker would debit shares from the seller's DEMAT account, hold them in the broker's pool account, and transfer them to the clearing corporation on T+2. Upon transfer, the client would receive a credit of funds against the sale, and the transaction would be considered settled. It was usual practice for brokers to debit shares on T day or T+1 day and transfer them to the clearing corporation on T+2 (since the settlement was on T+2).

From the time the shares were debited until they were settled, the client's shares lay in the broker's pool account, possibly allowing a broker to misuse these securities. SEBI identified this as a potential risk and introduced 'earmarking' for settlement. Under this system, shares are not immediately debited from the client's account upon selling. Instead, they are earmarked for settlement. Think of earmarking as a temporary hold on the securities towards an upcoming settlement for a sale transaction initiated by the client.

On settlement day, the earmarked shares are debited from the investor's account and credited to the clearing corporation. This new process eliminates the need for brokers to hold client shares in their pool accounts, thereby eliminating the risk.

The new earmarking process was made mandatory from November 2022.

Key takeaways

- The day you make a transaction is referred to as the trade date or T day.

- The broker must issue a contract note for all transactions by the end of T day.

- When you buy a share, it is credited to your DEMAT account by the end of T+1 day.

- All equity/stock settlements in India occur on a T+1 basis.

- When you sell shares, the shares are blocked immediately, and the sale proceeds are credited on T+1 day.

- Earmarking of shares was introduced to ensure that securities don't move out of the client's DEMAT account to the broker's pool account.

CHAPTER 11

Corporate Actions

When you invest in a stock, the primary objective is to benefit from stock price appreciation, also referred to as capital appreciation. A simple example of capital appreciation is when you invest in a stock at, say, ₹200, and after two years, you sell the same stock at ₹425. The capital appreciation in this case is ₹225 (i.e., ₹425 – ₹200).

In a sense, capital appreciation is the reward you get for the risk you've taken and the time you've given to your investment. That said, capital appreciation is not the only reward you can expect from holding a stock. Sometimes, you also benefit from corporate actions. Think of corporate actions as ways in which a company rewards its shareholders for being investors in the company. These rewards are financial in nature. Typically, a corporate action is initiated by the board of directors during board meetings or at the company's annual general meeting. Once discussed and ratified, the major shareholders should also give their consent.

As an investor, a good understanding of these corporate actions provides a clear picture of the company's financial health, which further helps when analysing a company for investment.

In this chapter, I'll help you understand the five most important corporate actions, their impact on stock prices and what they mean for you as an investor.

Dividends

Let's take a simple example. A company makes ₹100 crore in profits in a given financial year. Out of this ₹100 crore, the company decides to reinvest ₹80 crore back into the business—perhaps to upgrade machinery, expand plants or buy new manufacturing equipment. It also decides to retain ₹10 crore to manage operations. After provisioning ₹90 crore for these purposes, the company is left with ₹10 crore. It then decides to distribute this to its shareholders. Assume there are five equal shareholders in the company; each shareholder would receive ₹2 crore.

A few things to note:

- A portion of profits is distributed to shareholders.

- The decision to distribute profits is taken by the company's board of directors.

- If there are no profits, there would be nothing to distribute.

The portion of profits that the company distributes to its shareholders is called a dividend. It is a common practice for companies to give out dividends to their shareholders.

Dividends are paid on a per-share basis. For example, Infosys recently declared a dividend of ₹42 per share.

This means you get ₹42 as dividend income for every Infosys share you own. If you own 100 Infosys shares, you would receive ₹4,200 (100 x ₹42) as dividend income. The company directly remits the dividend to your bank account, which is linked to your DEMAT account.

Dividends are also expressed as a percentage of the face value. In the above example, Infosys has a face value of ₹5, and the dividend declared was ₹42. Hence, the dividend payout is said to be 840 per cent (₹42 ÷ ₹5).

It is not mandatory to pay dividends every year. If a company believes that instead of paying dividends to shareholders, they are better off utilizing the same cash to fund a new project for a better future, they can do so. Typically, companies in the high-growth phase prefer to plough profits back into the business rather than pay dividends.

However, when growth opportunities slow down and the company holds excess cash, it often makes sense to reward shareholders through dividends. Distributing surplus cash to shareholders through dividends can be a better use of capital than retaining the cash on the company's books.

Dividends need not be paid from profits alone. If a company has incurred losses during the year but holds healthy cash reserves, it can still pay dividends from those reserves.

The decision to pay a dividend and the amount to be paid is taken by the company's board members at the annual general meeting. Dividends are not paid immediately after they are announced. This is because shares are traded throughout the year, and it would be difficult to identify who is eligible to receive dividends and who isn't. The following timeline will help you understand the dividend cycle:

Dividend declaration date: This is the date on which the annual general meeting takes place, and the company's board approves the dividend issue.

Record date: This is the date on which the company reviews its shareholder register to identify eligible shareholders for the dividend. Usually, the time between the dividend declaration date and the record date is thirty days.

Ex-date/ex-dividend date: The ex-dividend date (or ex-date) is the cut-off date that determines who receives an upcoming dividend payment. If you buy the stock before the ex-date, you will receive the dividend. If you buy the stock on or after the ex-dividend date, you will not receive that particular dividend; the seller will get it instead.

For example, if a company announces a dividend with an ex-date of 5 December:

- Buy the stock on 4 December or earlier → you get the dividend

- Buy the stock on 5 December or later → you do not get the dividend

Remember, in the previous chapter we discussed the system of T+1 settlement in India. So, to be eligible for a dividend, you must ensure you buy the shares before the ex-dividend date.

Dividend payout date: This is the date on which dividends are paid to shareholders listed in the company register.

When a stock goes ex-dividend, its price usually drops by roughly the amount of the dividend paid. For example, if ITC is trading at ₹400 per share and declares a dividend of ₹20, the stock price will drop to around ₹380 on the ex-date. This happens because dividends paid are considered cash out. Hence the new stock price has to factor in the reduced balance sheet value, and the price drops.

That said, you will not always notice a significant drop in the share price. Larger and more noticeable price drops happen when a company announces a special dividend—a one-time, non-recurring dividend that is significantly larger than regular dividends. Such price drops should not be considered negative, as you will receive a cash payment as a shareholder.

Finally, dividends can be paid at any time during the financial year. Dividends paid during the year are called interim dividends, while dividends paid at the end of the financial year are called final dividends.

Bonus issue

Sometimes, a company may choose not to pay a dividend and instead issue bonus shares. Think of bonus shares as additional shares given to shareholders for every share they already own.

These 'free' share allotments typically come in fixed ratios such as 1:1, 2:1, 3:1 and so on. For example, if you own one share and the company announces a 1:1 bonus, you receive one additional share for every share you own. If the ratio is 2:1, existing shareholders get two additional shares for every share they hold, at no additional cost. So, if a shareholder owns 100 shares, 200 additional shares will be awarded.

This may seem very exciting at first, but there is a plot twist.

While the number of shares increases, the value of your investment remains the same. In a bonus issue, the stock price declines to the extent of the bonus ratio; however, this decline should not be mistaken for a correction or a fall in the stock price.

To illustrate this, let's take a few examples using different bonus ratios: 1:1, 3:1 and 5:1.

BONUS RATIOS

Bonus issue	No. of shares held before bonus	Share price before bonus issue (₹)	Value of investment (₹)	No. of shares held post bonus	Share price after bonus issue (₹)	Value of investment (₹)
1:1	100	75	7,500	200	37.5	7,500
3:1	30	550	16,500	120	137.5	16,500
5:1	2,000	15	30,000	12,000	2.5	30,000

Take the 5:1 bonus issue example—the ratio indicates you receive five shares for every one share you own. Before the bonus issue, you held 2,000 shares. After the bonus issue, the number of shares you hold increases to 12,000. Remember, 10,000 new shares are issued, while the original 2,000 shares remain unchanged, resulting in a total of 12,000 shares.

The share price, which was ₹15 per share, declines in the same proportion and becomes ₹2.5 per share. The total investment value (₹30,000) remains unchanged both before and after the bonus issue.

So, as you can see, in a bonus issue, only the number of shares increases, while the value of your investment remains the same.

The bonus announcement date, ex-bonus date and record date follow a timeline similar to that of a dividend issue.

Companies issue bonus shares to encourage retail participation, especially when a company's share price becomes very high, making it difficult for new investors to buy the stock. When bonus shares are issued, the number of outstanding shares increases and the share price is slashed, as shown in the earlier example.

Think about this for a moment—if a bonus issue does not actually increase the value of an investment, then why do companies do it at all? How does this reward investors?

Well, if a company's share price becomes very high— say ₹5,000 or ₹6,000 per share—fewer retail participants are able to buy or sell the stock. For example, the share price of MRF Limited is in the region of ₹1,52,000 per share. A retail investor has to shell out ₹1,52,000 to buy just one share. This also means a small retail investor with, say, ₹25,000 to invest can never buy MRF shares.

Having many retail investors spreads the risk across hundreds and thousands of investors as opposed to a few investors. Hence, when a stock price bloats, companies issue bonus shares to slash the stock price without impacting any other financial metric.

So why doesn't MRF split its shares? Well, at the end of the day, the decision rests solely with the company's management and board, and I guess MRF is yet to make up their mind, or perhaps they simply choose not to engage in such corporate actions. 😊

Stock split

The term 'stock split' may sound unusual, but it occurs regularly in the markets. What this means—quite literally—is that the stock you hold is split!

Similar to a bonus issue, when the company declares a stock split, the number of shares you hold increases, but the investment value remains the same. The big difference between a bonus issue and a stock split is that in a bonus issue, the face value of the company's shares remains unchanged, whereas in a stock split, the face value changes. For example, suppose a stock has a face value of ₹10, and there is a 1:2 stock split. After the split, the face value becomes ₹5. If you owned one share before the split, you would now own two shares after the split.

We will illustrate this with an example:

SPLIT RATIO

Split ratio	Face value (₹)	No. of shares held before split	Share price before split (₹)	Value of investment (₹)	New face value (₹)	No of shares post-split	Share price after split (₹)	Value of investment (₹)
1:2	10	100	900	90,000	5	200	450	90,000
1:5	10	100	900	90,000	2	500	180	90,000

Like a bonus issue, a stock split encourages more retail participation by reducing the price per share. The dates and timeline—announcement date, ex-date, record date and so on—are similar to those for dividends and bonus issues.

Rights issue

The goal of a rights issue is to raise fresh capital. However, instead of going public, the company approaches its existing shareholders. Think about a rights issue as a second IPO, but one that is offered only to a select group of people, namely, existing shareholders.

A rights issue could indicate a promising new development in the company, but this is not always the case. As an investor, you must evaluate the reasons for the rights issue and determine if it makes sense.

Shareholders can subscribe to the rights issue in proportion to their shareholding. For example, a 1:4 rights issue means that for every four shares held, a shareholder can subscribe to one additional share. Shares offered under a rights issue are issued at a discount to the prevailing market price. For example, if a stock is trading at ₹500 per share, the rights issue price could be set at a 20 per cent discount, at ₹400 per share.

However, a word of caution—investors should not be swayed by the discount on offer and must look beyond it. A rights issue is different from a bonus issue as one is paying money to acquire shares. Hence, shareholders should subscribe only if they are fully convinced about the company's future.

It is also possible that after a rights issue is announced, the stock price may fall below the rights issue price. If the market price drops below the subscription price/rights issue price, it is cheaper to buy it from the open market.

Share buyback

A buyback can be seen as a company's way of investing in itself by buying its own shares from investors in the market. A buyback reduces the number of shares outstanding in the market; it also serves as an important corporate restructuring method. There can be many reasons why companies choose to buy back shares:

- To improve profitability on a per-share basis
- To consolidate their stake in the company
- To prevent a potential takeover
- To signal promoter confidence in the company
- To support the share price from declining in the markets

When a company announces a buyback, it signals confidence in its own business prospects. Hence, this is usually positive for the share price, but like other things in the market, always evaluate the reasons behind the corporate action.

Key takeaways

- Corporate actions have an impact on stock prices.

- Dividends are a means of rewarding shareholders and are announced as a percentage of the face value.

- You must own a company's stock before the ex-dividend date to be eligible for the dividend.

- A bonus issue is a form of stock dividend and is the company's way of rewarding shareholders with additional shares.

- A stock split is based on face value; both the face value and stock price change in proportion to the split ratio.

- A rights issue allows a company to raise fresh capital from existing shareholders. Subscribe to it only if you think it makes sense.

- A buyback signals promoter confidence and conveys optimism about the company's prospects.

CHAPTER 12

Key Market Events

In Chapter 6, we understood that stock prices move constantly and that company-specific news tends to influence these movements. We also learned that external events—both economic and non-economic—can impact stocks and the market's performance in general. Some of these events are recurring in nature, while others are unpredictable. A good example of an unpredictable event that had a significant negative impact on stock prices is the COVID-19 pandemic.

In this chapter, we will try to understand some common recurring events and how the stock market reacts to them.

Monetary policy

Monetary policy is a tool through which a central bank controls the money supply by controlling interest rates. The Reserve Bank of India (RBI) is India's central bank. Likewise, every country has a central bank responsible for setting interest rates. For example, the European Central Bank in Europe and the Federal Reserve in the United States. Central banks adjust interest rates to control money supply in the mainstream economy.

While setting interest rates, the RBI must strike a balance between growth and inflation. In a nutshell, when interest rates are high, borrowing rates are high—particularly for corporations. If companies can't borrow easily, they cannot expand, and if they don't expand, economic growth slows down.

On the other hand, when interest rates are low, borrowing becomes easier. This translates to more money in the hands of corporations and consumers. With more money, there is increased spending, which means sellers tend to increase the prices of goods and services, leading to inflation.

To strike a balance, the RBI considers multiple economic factors and carefully sets the key rates. Any imbalance in these rates can lead to economic chaos.

The key RBI rates you need to track are as follows:

Repo rate: Private and public sector banks (such as ICICI, HDFC and SBI), also referred to as commercial banks, can borrow from the RBI. The rate at which the RBI lends money to other banks is called the repo rate. When the repo rate is high, the cost of borrowing is high, leading to slow economic growth. You can check the latest repo rate on the RBI's website. Markets don't like an increase in the repo rate because higher borrowing costs tend to slow down growth.

Reverse repo rate: This is the rate at which the RBI borrows from commercial banks. When banks have excess funds, they can lend this money to the RBI for a short period (usually overnight) and earn interest at the reverse repo rate. This provides banks with a safe, low-risk way to park surplus cash.

The RBI (or any central bank) uses the reverse repo rate as a tool to control the money supply in the banking system. When the central bank wants to reduce liquidity in the economy—often to control inflation—it can increase the reverse repo rate. This encourages banks to lend more money to the central bank rather than to businesses or consumers, effectively pulling money out of circulation.

Conversely, when the central bank lowers the reverse repo rate, banks are less incentivized to park money with it and may instead lend more to the public, increasing liquidity in the economy.

Cash reserve ratio (CRR): Every bank must maintain a certain amount of funds with the RBI. This amount is dependent on the CRR. If the CRR increases, more money is sucked out of the mainstream economy, which is not good for economic activity.

The monetary policy committee meets regularly to review the economic situation and decide upon these key rates. Therefore, keeping track of monetary policy announcements is a must for any active trader. The first to react to rate decisions are typically interest-rate-sensitive stocks across various sectors such as banking, automobiles, housing finance, real estate and metals.

The RBI meets bi-monthly to review policy rates and make changes, if any. Stock market participants eagerly wait for the central bank's monetary policy decisions as these often influence stock price movement.

Inflation

Inflation is a sustained increase in the general prices of goods and services. Increasing inflation erodes the purchasing power of money. All things being equal, if the cost of 1 kg of onions increases from ₹15 to ₹20, this price rise is attributed to inflation.

Inflation is inevitable, but a high inflation rate is undesirable as it could lead to economic uneasiness. A high level of inflation tends to send a negative signal to markets. Both the government and the RBI work towards keeping inflation at manageable levels.

Inflation is typically measured using an index. If the inflation index increases by a certain percentage, it indicates rising inflation. Conversely, when the index declines, it indicates that inflation is cooling off.

There are two inflation indices: The wholesale price index (WPI) and the consumer price index (CPI).

WPI: The WPI indicates price movements at the wholesale level. It captures the price change when goods are bought and sold in bulk. WPI is an easy and convenient method to calculate inflation. However, the inflation measured here is at an institutional level and does not necessarily capture the inflation experienced by end consumers.

CPI: The CPI, on the other hand, captures the effect of price changes at the retail level. As a consumer, CPI inflation is what matters. The calculation of CPI is quite detailed as it involves classifying consumption into various categories and subcategories across urban and rural regions. Each of these categories is converted into an index; the final CPI index is a composite of several individual indices. The CPI captures the effect of inflation on daily household consumables such as fruits, vegetables and cereals, as well as fuels like petrol and diesel.

The computation of CPI is quite rigorous and detailed. It is one of the most critical metrics for studying the economy. The Ministry of Statistics and Programme Implementation (MOSPI) publishes CPI data around the second week of every month.

A key challenge for the RBI is to strike a balance between inflation and interest rates. Usually, a low interest rate tends to increase inflation, while a high interest rate tends to arrest inflation.

Index of industrial production

The index of industrial production (IIP) is a short-term indicator of growth in the country's industrial sector. The data is released every month (along with inflation data) by the Ministry of Statistics and Programme Implementation (MOSPI). As the name suggests, the IIP measures production levels in India's industrial sector against a fixed reference point, known as the base year. Currently, India uses 2011–12 as the base year.

Roughly fifteen different industries submit their production data to the ministry, which collates the information and releases it as an index number. An increase in the IIP indicates a vibrant industrial environment, as production is going up, and is hence a positive sign for the economy and markets. A decline in the IIP points to a sluggish production environment, which is a negative sign for the economy and markets.

In summary, an upswing in industrial production is good for the economy, while a downturn rings an alarm. As India becomes more industrialized, the relative importance of the IIP continues to increase.

A lower IIP number puts pressure on the RBI to lower interest rates to aid industry through cheaper credit.

Purchasing managers' index

The purchasing managers' index (PMI) is an economic indicator that captures business activity across the country's manufacturing and service sectors. It is a survey-based indicator in which respondents—typically purchasing managers—report changes in business conditions compared with the previous month.

Separate surveys are conducted for the service and manufacturing sectors. The data from these surveys are consolidated on a single index. Typical areas covered in the survey include new orders, output, business expectations and employment.

The PMI usually oscillates around the fifty mark. A reading above fifty indicates expansion, while a reading below fifty signals a contraction in the economy. A reading of exactly fifty indicates no change.

Budget

A budget is an event during which the Ministry of Finance presents the country's finances in detail. The finance minister, on behalf of the ministry, makes a budget presentation to the nation. During the budget, major policy initiatives and economic reforms are announced, which impact various industries across the markets. Therefore, the budget plays a vital role in the economy and has a big impact on stock prices.

To illustrate this, in a recent budget, duties on cigarettes were expected to increase. As anticipated, the finance minister raised these duties, leading to an increase in cigarette prices. Higher cigarette prices can have several implications:

- Increased prices may discourage smokers from buying cigarettes (needless to say, this is debatable), which can decrease the profitability of cigarette manufacturing companies such as ITC.

- If profitability declines, investors may want to sell shares of ITC.

- If market participants start selling ITC shares, the market can decline because ITC is a heavyweight stock in the index.

In reaction to this budget announcement, ITC traded 7.5 per cent lower.

The Union Budget is an annual event, typically announced in February. However, the budget announcement could be delayed under certain special circumstances, such as the formation of a new government.

Corporate earnings announcement

The corporate earnings season is perhaps one of the most important events to which stock prices react. Listed companies must declare their earnings once every quarter, also referred to as quarterly earnings results.

During an earnings announcement, a company provides details on various operational and financial activities, including:

- Revenue growth
- Expense trends
- Finance charges
- Profitability trends
- Project updates
- Key industry trends

In addition, some companies provide an overview of what to expect from the upcoming months, both in terms of business operations and financials. This forecast is called 'corporate guidance'.

The table below gives you an overview of the earnings season in India:

No.	Months	Quarter	Results announcement
1	April–June	Quarter 1 (Q1)	1st week of July
2	July–September	Quarter 2 (Q2)	1st week of October
3	October–December	Quarter 3 (Q3)	1st week of January
4	January–March	Quarter 4 (Q4)	1st week of April

Do note that in India, the financial year begins on 1 April. In the US, the financial year starts on 1 January, so the first quarter runs from January through March, and so forth.

Each time a company declares its quarterly earnings, market participants compare the reported numbers against what they had expected the company to earn. These expectations are referred to as 'street expectations'.

If the company's earnings are better than street expectations, the stock price will react positively. If the numbers are lower than street expectations, the stock price will react negatively.

If actual earnings match expectations, the stock tends to trade flat, sometimes with a negative bias, as the company did not give a positive surprise.

You may find it interesting that invariably, every quarter, Infosys is the first big company to make the quarterly announcement. They also regularly give out guidance. Market participants follow Infosys's guidance as it impacts the markets; this sets the tone for the IT sector as a whole.

Non-financial events

Apart from the events discussed above, it is also important to watch out for non-financial events and understand their impact on the markets. For example, the Covid crisis of 2020 had a significant effect on economies around the world, disrupting the global economic order. Supply chains took a hit worldwide, leading to an inflation spike. That said, there were select pockets of the economy that did very well, mainly the online services industry.

Geopolitical events such as the Russia–Ukraine war or tensions between China and Taiwan have impacted global markets. Such developments affect interconnected economies. For instance, the war between Russia and Ukraine has disrupted the supply of natural gas and crude oil, significantly impacting energy costs in Europe.

While global economies are interconnected, country-specific events impact the local economy. For example, the elections in India impact primarily the Indian economy.

As an active trader or market participant, you need to watch out for these events and understand how they can influence the markets or specific industries.

Key takeaways

- Markets and individual stocks react to events. Market participants should equip themselves to understand and interpret these events.

- Monetary policy is one of the most important economic events. During monetary policy reviews, actions on repo, reverse repo, cash reserve ratio, etc. are initiated.

- Interest rates and inflation are related. Increasing interest rates curbs inflation and lowering interest rates can fuel inflation.

- The Ministry of Statistics and Programme Implementation releases inflation data every month. As a consumer, consumer price index inflation data is the most relevant metric to track.

- The index of industrial production measures industrial activity. An increase in IIP cheers the markets, while a decline disappoints the market.

- The purchasing managers' index is a survey-based business sentiment indicator. The PMI oscillates around the fifty mark. Above fifty is good news to the markets, while a PMI below fifty is not.

- The Union Budget is an important market event during which policy announcements and reform initiatives are introduced. Markets and stocks react strongly to budget announcements.

- Corporate earnings are reported every quarter. Stocks react mainly due to the difference between actual results and street expectations.

- Keep an eye on non-financial events and how they can impact the markets.

CHAPTER 13

Dig Deeper

Congratulations! If you've read all the chapters in this book, it means you don't just have a passing interest in stock markets but rather a genuine desire to learn, invest and create wealth through the market.

I'd say you are now warmed up to dig deeper.

The objective of this book was to give you a quick, hands-on introduction to the stock markets. In this effort, I have carefully selected concepts that are essential, especially if you are new to the markets. At this stage, it's actually a good sign if you are left with many unanswered questions. I'm sure you will find those answers as you start digging deeper into the world of stock markets.

Before we wrap up, it's important to understand that from here, there are many learning pathways you can pursue. Think of each pathway as a stock market topic. All these pathways are interrelated. Some of them are:

- Technical analysis
- Fundamental analysis
- Futures trading
- Option theory
- Option strategies
- Markets and taxation
- Commodity trading

- Risk management and trading philosophy
- Trading systems
- Mutual funds
- Financial modelling

This list can go on, and learning about stock markets can be a lifelong endeavour. I've been at it for the last two decades, and I still have miles to go.

How are they connected?

I've listed several stock market topics above, and I mentioned that they are all interrelated. You may now be wondering how each topic connects with the others. To help you gain some perspective, let me ask you a question. To be successful in the markets, what, according to you, is the single most important factor?

Success in the markets can be easily defined: If you make money consistently, you are successful.

So, going back to the question: What is the single most important factor for success in the stock markets?

If you were to answer this, chances are you would think of risk management, discipline, market timing, access to information and so on. While one cannot deny the importance of these factors, developing a point of view (POV) is even more compelling and fundamental.

A point of view is the ability to form a sense of direction on a stock or an index. If you believe a stock is likely to go up, your POV is bullish, and you would be a buyer of the stock. If you believe a stock is likely to go down, your POV is bearish, and you would be a seller of the stock.

Without a POV, you won't know what to do in the market. Once you develop a POV, you can add other elements such as risk management, timing and macro and micro factors to improve the odds of your trade. But without a POV, you can't even get started. For this reason, I consider developing a POV to be the most important factor in market success.

Having said that, how do you develop a point of view? How do you figure out whether a stock is going up or down?

To develop a POV, one needs a systematic approach to analysing the markets. A few of the methods used to analyse what to buy or sell are:

- Fundamental analysis (FA)

- Technical analysis (TA)

- Quantitative analysis (QA)

- Outside views

To give you a preview, here is a typical illustration of a trader's thought process while developing a POV (whether to buy or sell stock) using different methods of analysis:

- **FA-based POV:** The company's quarterly numbers look impressive. IT has reported 25 per cent top-line and 15 per cent bottom-line growth. The company's guidance also looks positive. When all the fundamental factors are aligned, the stock looks bullish; hence, the stock is a buy.

- **TA-based POV:** A technical analyst will derive his or her point of view by analysing the stock price charts. Here is an example of how it sounds: The moving average convergence and divergence (MACD) indicator has turned bullish along with a bullish engulfing candlestick pattern. The stock is also trading at its support point. Based on this analysis, the short-term sentiment looks positive; therefore, the stock can be considered a good buy.

- **QA-based POV:** A quantitative analyst will derive his or her point of view by looking at the stock price purely from a mathematical lens. A typical point of view sounds like this: Following a recent up move, the stock's price-to-earnings (P/E) ratio has touched the third standard deviation. There is only a 1 per cent probability of the P/E breaching this level. Hence, it is prudent to expect mean reversion; therefore, the stock is a sell.

- **Outside view:** An analyst on television recommends a buy on the stock; therefore, the stock is a buy.

The POV you take should always be based on your own analysis rather than an outsider's view, as more often than not, one regrets acting solely on an external view.

So, after developing a POV, what do you do next? Do you immediately buy or sell the stock and act on that POV? This is where the complexity of markets starts to kick in.

If your POV is bullish, you can choose to do one of the following:

- Buy the stock in the spot market.

- Buy the stock in the derivatives markets.

- Within derivatives, you can choose to buy futures.

- Trade through the options market.

- Within the options market, choose between call options and put options.

- Combine call and put options to create a synthetic bullish trade.

What you choose to do after developing a POV is a different ball game altogether. Selecting the right instrument that complements your POV is critical to profitable trading.

For example, if I'm extremely bullish on a stock from a one-year perspective, I'm better off making a delivery trade. However, if I'm bullish from a short-term perspective—say, one week—I'd rather choose a futures instrument to trade.

If I'm bullish with constraints attached (for example, I expect the markets to bounce after a great budget announcement but don't want to risk too much), it would be prudent to choose an option instrument.

The key takeaway is this: a market participant should develop a point of view and complement that POV with the right trading instrument. A well-researched POV combined with the right instrument is a perfect recipe for success in the markets.

By now, you should also have a sense of how the different learning pathways I mentioned earlier play an important part in understanding the stock markets in a holistic manner.

Point of view flowchart

This helps you understand how to think about your market participation from your point of view. For example, if you develop your point of view from fundamental analysis, then you execute that point of view by logging into a trading terminal and making a spot market transaction or in simple terms an investment.

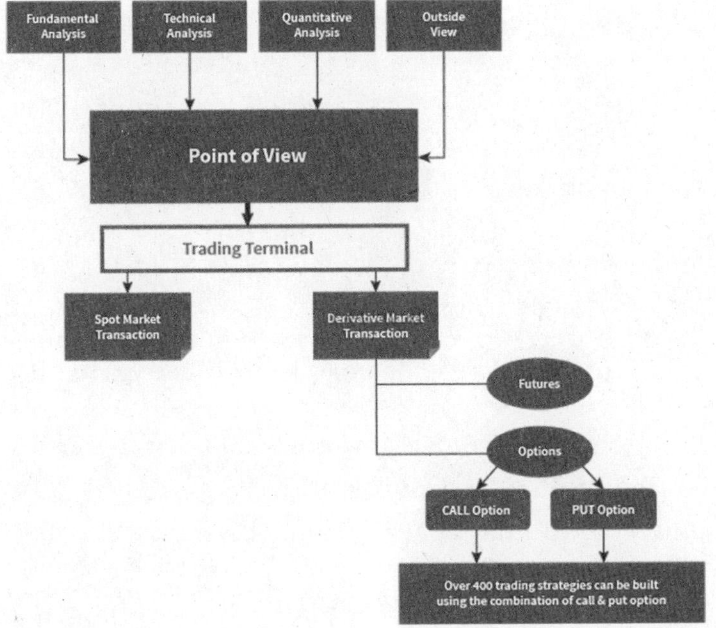

There are multiple decision-making points, and each one has an impact on your P&L.

With this in mind, go ahead and explore the stock markets! Pick up topics that interest you and start learning more about them. With everything you've learned so far, begin with small investments and start experiencing the wealth-creation process. This is how your stock market journey truly begins.

I hope you enjoy it as much as I do.

About the Author

Karthik Rangappa is Chief of Education Services at Zerodha Broking Limited. He is the creator of the Zerodha Varsity programme, which is Zerodha's flagship learning portal.